EISENHOWER

AN AMERICAN HERO

EISENHOWER
AN AMERICAN HERO

THE HISTORICAL RECORD OF HIS LIFE

by

THE EDITORS OF
AMERICAN HERITAGE MAGAZINE

and

UNITED PRESS INTERNATIONAL

Introduction by

BRUCE CATTON

Biographical Narrative by

KENNETH S. DAVIS

AMERICAN HERITAGE/BONANZA BOOKS
New York

Printed in Italy.

This 1984 edition is published by Bonanza Books, distributed by Crown
Publishers, Inc., by arrangement with American Heritage Publishing Co.

ISBN 0-517-45114X

h g f e d c b a

INTRODUCTION

By BRUCE CATTON

More than any other position in America the Presidency is a job for a politician. Most of the time the electorate recognizes that fact and chooses a man who has had experience and shown capacity in the political field. To be sure, a good military reputation is no drawback, and a politician who has been a good soldier is apt to find that his candidacy is made more appealing thereby—as witness the cases (to name just two) of Andrew Jackson and Theodore Roosevelt. But military reputation usually is no more than the icing on the cake. It may please the voters, but the voters pick their man primarily because he is a good politician. They elect presidents, not generals.

Twice, however, it has happened the other way. Twice the electorate went entirely outside of politics and chose as President a man who was a professional soldier pure and simple—a man who never before ran for office or took any part in politics and who made his entire reputation as a military man. Two West Pointers, and only two, have lived in the White House: General Ulysses S. Grant, elected in 1868, and General Dwight D. Eisenhower, elected in 1952. Here are two great departures from the strongest tradition in American politics.

The departures reflect the times in which they were made. In each case the nation was trying to recover from a war which it had hoped to avoid and which it had trouble understanding. Something incomprehensible had been won, at enormous cost, but nameless perils obviously lay ahead, and it seemed possible that what had been won might easily be lost. Both the immediate past and the ominous future appeared to be at stake, and it was necessary to do something drastic about it.

The great tradition is fractured, in short, when the people are desperate. They fracture it because they want to transcend politics; in other words, when they want to transcend themselves, politics being nothing less than a faithful transcription of the American spirit. To say that at such a moment the people are blindly trying to dodge their troubles by exalting a "father image" is mostly to utter wind-blown nonsense, but they unquestionably are both tired and worried, and they look for someone who, without making too many words about it, can preserve what has been won and restore the wartime vision without also restoring the wartime tension. This may be a hopeless quest, but it is not just an attempt to evade responsibility. It is an attempt to live up to something, if only by finding the man who can provide a breathing spell in which the nation can appraise what it has done and see what ought to be done next. And at such a moment the supremely successful soldier naturally looks like the man who is needed.

Note that it is the nonpolitical soldier who is chosen. The electorate passes over the leaders like General George B. McClellan and General Douglas MacArthur, each of whom, in addition to a notable military record, had the gift of eloquence and an undeniable knack for political maneuvering. Instead the nation turns, as if by instinct, to men who were soldiers and nothing else. The very lack of political experience looks like an asset, and the inability to be eloquent becomes precisely the quality the country wants most. The chosen soldiers are chosen because in some way they seem to represent the national average made larger than life-size. By their very silence and their devotion to duty they somehow express a let's-get-on-with-it spirit that is invaluable.

This may be fine for the electorate, but it is rather rough on the man who is chosen. Into the most completely political job on earth is thrust a man whose chief qualification is that he has no political background whatever. Trained for one job, the new President finds himself in a place for which his training is of no use whatever. He is apt to be judged by standards that have nothing to do with the reasons for his election—what was his legislative program, how much of it did he get through Congress, whom did he appoint to what jobs, how did his appointees behave, and in general what sort of leadership did he provide? These matters may be important, and yet in a way they are irrelevant. What the nation really wants, when it elects a Grant or an Eisenhower, is simply that the man elected continue to be what he was before he was elected—a national hero who somehow embodies in time of peace the national ideals he stood for in time of war.

This of course is an impossible assignment, because when a great war ends we demobilize our wartime ideals with a haste almost as frantic as the haste with which we demobilize our armed forces. The chosen hero is not given much to work with. There is bound to be a letdown, and when it comes we have a smug way of assuming that the President has been at fault. We blame him for our own shortcomings, and after a while we return to the familiar world of unadorned politics and let the hero make his way to Valhalla as best he can.

While he is going there his image is apt to become a little blurred, and it takes us a long time to get it back into focus. Eventually, however, we begin to see things more clearly, and as we do we may realize that the instinct that led us to elect him was a good deal sounder than the criticism we at last brought to bear on him. For what we actually asked of the chosen hero was that he preside over the affairs of a restless and impatient people who longed to get back to a vanished era when life was less complicated and frightening and who finally had to understand that getting back is impossible and that the strange new world has to be faced. In all of this

the hero could do little more than provide a feeling of security and confidence. The profound adjustment that had to come was one which we, the people, had to make for ourselves. The man at the top could give us time to make it, and an awareness that the adjustment was in fact inevitable, but the rest was up to us.

So now, when we take a final look at Dwight Eisenhower, we stand in judgment of ourselves as much as of him; and we find that the record is a good deal better than we have sometimes supposed. For the nation did, after all, get through the terribly difficult postwar transition without making the disastrous mistakes that could so easily have been made. We did not repeat the tragic error of the 1920's and try to take refuge in an unattainable isolation, letting the rest of the world go off to chaos in its own way. We evolved and put into operation a working philosophy of the unity of free peoples everywhere. We assumed leadership of the most portentous movement in recent centuries—the great drive toward a world order which has to be attained if human liberty and civilization itself are to survive. We were indeed guilty of a good deal of fumbling and backsliding along the way, but in the main the record is extremely good. Perhaps the best way to sum it up is to say that the ideals we fought for in the Second World War are still alive and that we are firmly committed to them.

It would of course be overstating the case to say that all of this was due to Eisenhower. But it would be equally wrong to assume that all of it would have happened without him. He was a part of it, and a very large part. He gave us the strength of a great reputation, a great character, and an abiding sense of America's mission; gave us, when all is said and done, the chance to live up to the best there is in us. Not very many Presidents have ever given us more.

A wagon rigged with an umbrella rumbles into the main street of a Kansas town, breaking the stillness of a sun-drenched summer day. The photograph was taken in 1910—a year before Ike left Abilene.

I

THE MAKING
OF A SOLDIER

On a golden June day, 1911, in the little Kansas town of Abilene, just a few miles from the exact geographical center of the United States, a young man was leaving home for the first time to make his way in the great world. Nothing especially distinguished him from thousands of other young men who were doing the same thing that summer across the length and breadth of America. He was somewhat older than most of these, being only four months short of voting age; but in other respects he was so well within the average for his time and place—in appearance, in opinions, in the quality of his attainments and the nature of his ambitions— that he could pass almost as the type of small-town, middle-class, Middle-Western American.

In early afternoon he stood at an upstairs window of his home, a plain white two-story frame house, numbered 201 South East Fourth Street, in the southeast corner of the town. He experienced such emotions as thousands of others felt that same summer, and for the same reason, as he looked out upon familiar scenes, saying good-by to them. He saw the grounds and the building of Lincoln School, where he had gone through the grades. He saw the house of the proprietor of a downtown café where he had loafed through many an hour. And beyond the house he saw open country—fields of knee-high corn and ripening wheat that flowed like sea waves in the wind, bounded in the distance by a green wall of willows and cottonwoods along the bank of the Smoky Hill River where he had swum in summer and skated in winter, year after year.

Then, through the window, across miles of open prairie to the west, he heard the sad lonely whistle of an approaching Union Pacific train. He seized his heavy suitcase and rushed downstairs.

On the front porch, beside a trellis on which red roses bloomed and through which could be seen the large vegetable garden he had helped plant and tend that year, as he had every year for almost as long as he could remember, he said good-by to his mother, his youngest brother, his dog Flip. (He had said good-by to his father and three of his brothers when they left for work that morning.) There was a moment of red-faced embarrassment for the young man. His twelve-year-old brother burst into unexpected tears; but his mother remained dry-eyed as she kissed her departing son (later she went upstairs and sobbed heartbrokenly), whereupon the

In 1867 the first trainload of cattle was shipped from Abilene. The engraving above right commemorated the eventful day that made Abilene a key cattle-shipping center for the next five years. In the Eisenhower family a date some ten years later was more important. Jacob Eisenhower, his family, and fellow members of a religious sect called the River Brethren migrated in 1878 from Pennsylvania to Kansas. A meeting of this pacifist sect, for which Jacob was a minister, is shown in the engraving above. Jacob's son David showed no interest in farming, his family's traditional vocation. Instead, in 1885, with the financial backing of his father, he opened a general store (right) in the town of Hope, Kansas.

young man again seized his suitcase and walked swiftly north toward the depot. Not once did he look back.

All this is standard Americana of a half-century ago, having of itself alone only a nostalgic value. But to impart to the scene a historical interest, and even a considerable historical importance, we need only speak the young man's name—Dwight David Eisenhower—and know that he left his home town, that bright June afternoon, to enter upon his plebe year at West Point. What we witness then is the opening of a career that would lead ultimately into positions of the greatest power and glory possible for anyone of this young man's generation—moreover, into a career that would measure and test a mind, a character, already essentially formed by this day of home-town leave-taking. To the end, Dwight Eisenhower as a human being could be accurately and fairly adequately defined in terms of the influences that had played upon him in Abilene, Kansas, at the turn of the century—influences classifiable under the two headings of family and local environment.

The earliest American Eisenhowers (they then spelled the name "Eisenhauer") came to Pennsylvania with a party of Mennonites from Europe in 1741. They settled among a community of German coreligionists along the banks of the Susquehanna, a location that caused the sect to become known as the River Brethren. There the family remained for more than a century and a quarter.

Most of the Eisenhowers were farmers. But one of them, Frederick, born in 1794, became a highly skilled weaver who "prospered with his looms" and enhanced his prosperity by marrying a Barbara dan Miller of Millersburg who (she was five years his elder) brought him a "very generous dowry." They raised six children to maturity, of whom one, Jacob, born in 1828, became a minister as well as a farmer and who was generally acknowledged to be the outstanding member of his family's generation. Jacob "prospered with his acres," as his father had with his looms, and, like his father, he married a woman somewhat older than he who brought a generous dowry. Her name was Rebecca Matter and she was of the River Brethren. Rebecca became the mother of fourteen children, only six of whom lived to maturity.

One of the six, born in 1863, was christened David. He was among four of Jacob's children (a daughter and three sons) who emigrated with their parents from Pennsylvania to Dickinson County, Kansas, in the spring of 1878. They came as part of a River Brethren colony numbering something over two hundred. Jacob Eisenhower was among the colony's leaders. And in Kansas, on a farm of rich alluvial soil, he prospered. A measure of his prosperity was his standard wedding gift to each of his children: a 160-acre farm and two thousand dollars in cash. This gift became young David's when, on September 23, 1885 (his twenty-second birthday), in the chapel of a now long-defunct educational institution called Lane University, operated by the United Brethren Church in Lecompton, Kansas, he married Ida Elizabeth Stover.

She too was of German Mennonite stock, she was a year and five months older than her husband, and she brought to him a dowry. Thus far did David follow the marriage pattern established by his father and grandfather. Ida Stover had been born and raised, however, not in Pennsylvania but in Virginia's Shenandoah Valley; her inheritance was a meager one, and she possessed a more independent, self-assertive spirit than was evidently common among the women the Eisenhowers married.

Ida's enrollment at Lane in the fall of 1883 was a demonstration of her spirit, since orthodox members of her sect did not look with favor upon higher education for women. It had also used up a considerable portion of the slender inheritance from her father. The remainder was brought to her young husband with her marriage vows and was promptly lost by him, along with his own more substantial inheritance, in a disastrous business venture.

David had been a quiet, moody, introverted child who early learned to loathe the physical drudgery of farm life. The only part of it he liked was the handling and repair of machinery. His ambition when he entered Lane was to become a mechanical engineer, although Lane's limited curriculum was not such as to help him realize it. And engineering remained his favorite career choice even when, faced with the necessity to support a wife, he formed a business partnership with another newly married young man. In the fall of 1885 they opened a general-merchandise store in Hope, Kansas, a tiny village a few miles south of Abilene.

Three years later the business failed. There were charges, never formally lodged, and much less proved, of dishonesty by David's partner. There was the undeniable fact of negligence and poor judgment by David himself. The upshot was that he fled precipitously and ignominiously from the scene of his humiliation, leaving behind in Hope (ironic name!) an infant son named Arthur and a wife who again was pregnant. He went to Denison, Texas, where he worked in the shops of the Cotton Belt Railroad for less than forty dollars a month. His family joined him there early in 1889.

He was by that time the father of a second son, Edgar, born in January of the new year. His third, the one through whom the family name was destined to become one of the most famous in the world, was born on October 14, 1890, in the small multigabled house David had rented by the railroad tracks. His mother named him David Dwight—the name was written D. Dwight in the family Bible—but she began early to call him by his middle name because it was confusing to have two Davids in the family. Also, she disliked nicknames: it annoyed her that Arthur became "Art" and Edgar "Ed," and she was determined her third son would be known by his "right" name. But the right name for an Eisenhower is "Ike," as Edgar's schoolmates quickly discovered, and so he was called through his school years. He became "Big Ike" and his next younger brother "Little Ike" as soon as the latter entered school.

This did not occur in Texas, however, but back in Abilene. David's brother-in-law, Chris Musser, was named foreman in 1890 of the Belle Springs Creamery, a prosperous commercial enterprise launched years before by the River Brethren. He offered David the job of plant "engineer." David promptly accepted, moving his family in the spring of 1891. He remained a Belle Springs employee for twenty years at a wage never as high as one hundred dollars a month—on the low side even for those days. To raise six healthy sons to maturity on such an income (he and Ida had seven sons,

Ike's parents lean against a carved prop (above) for a photograph to commemorate their wedding day, September 23, 1885. The new Mrs. Eisenhower, formerly Ida Elizabeth Stover, and her husband met the year before as students at Lane University.

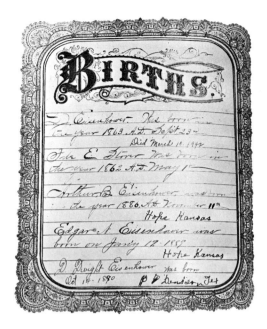

In the family Bible, on the bottom of a page marked "Births," Ida Eisenhower recorded the arrival of her third son, D. (for David) Dwight. Later on, the names were reversed to eliminate confusion between father and son. Below, the Eisenhower boys, then five in number, pose before the Victorian cottage that was their first home in Abilene. Dwight stands at far left.

one of whom died in infancy) required near miracles of home organization, industry, and management.

These near miracles were the mother's. Under heavy pressure, Ida demonstrated elements of genuine greatness—a character of unusual strength, a personality of unusual sweetness, an administrative ability of the first order. When the family moved from an outgrown rented house to the larger one on South East Fourth Street—a house at first rented but later bought from David's younger brother—Ida was the one who calculated how every bit of the new property, including a large barn and three adjoining acres of fertile land, could be used to best advantage. Under her supervision the Eisenhowers raised nearly all their own food, with a surplus for cash sale, a good portion of such sales being by market wagon through the streets of the town. She was the true head of the family. Yet she scrupulously maintained all the forms of the traditional German patriarchy. She encouraged her husband to make decisions by which she must abide. She insisted that he handle the finances. She impressed upon her children the ruling power of their father's wish. He it was who sat at the head of the table and said grace at mealtime—and led the family Bible readings.

These last were weekly sessions, and lengthy ones, designed to reinforce the teachings of Sunday school in the River Brethren meetinghouse, which was invariably attended by the whole family. For, insofar as the parents could establish the central theme of family life, and of the life of each growing son, that theme was religious; the religion was a primitive Christianity that was frankly, even proudly, proclaimed as such.

During the dark months of their Texas exile, amidst bitterness and despair, David and Ida had turned to the Scriptures for consolation. Studying these as never before, they had moved much further in the direction of Christian primitivism than most River Brethren were willing to go. By the time they had returned to Kansas, they were ripe for conversion, if not already converted, to the beliefs of a Fundamentalist sect later known as Jehovah's Witnesses, whose members became notorious for the persistence of their proselyting efforts and for their refusal to register for military service—their refusal even to salute the flag.

All this had its effect upon Dwight and the other Eisenhower sons while they were growing up. It was an effect difficult now to assess. Certainly it differed from that which the mother and father hoped to achieve. None of the boys turned out to be devout. On the contrary, each seems to have rebelled against the excessive and intensely boring Bible reading and discussion to which he was subjected as a child. Dwight, for instance, would have no church affiliation whatever—he would rarely so much as attend a church service—through the greater part of his adult life. Nor did the parents' religious extremism interfere at all with the normal, healthy development of the sons in relation to each other and to the world at large. The parental religion had at its core a respect for the individual as a creature of God who, endowed with free will, could choose (and must himself alone make the choice) between good and evil. David and Ida insisted that each of their sons be fully exposed to it; beyond that, they believed, their right did not extend.

Dwight Eisenhower, in overalls and a calico shirt (first row, second from left), poses with his fifth-grade classmates in 1900 on the steps of Abilene's Lincoln School. In this same building Ike went through his first six grades. For his junior high school years he entered Garfield School across the tracks on the "good" (north) side of town. Before and after school hours, Ike and his brothers were expected to do their daily chores at home. These included tending the livestock and the gardens. When each of the Eisenhower boys was old enough, he supplemented the family income by working at the prosperous Belle Springs Creamery, where their father was already employed as a mechanic. The original building (at right) had long since been replaced by a large brick structure by the time Dwight took a permanent job there in 1909.

Dwight's contemporaries escape the Kansas summer heat with a swim in Mud Creek.

A husky, sports-minded youth, Ike organized Abilene High's athletic association in 1908 and served as its first president. He was a competent end on the school's football team and played right field on the baseball team (shown below, with Ike in the center of the first row). Also an avid hunter and fisherman, he took frequent camping trips (like the one pictured at left). From Abilene High School he received in 1909 the rococo diploma at lower left.

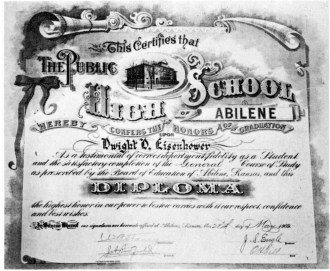

The same laissez-faire attitude extended to other aspects of their sons' lives. Each boy worked for wages in the Belle Springs Creamery as soon as he was old enough to be employed, and each was therefore respected as an economically independent person while yet in his teens. The parents felt they had no right to interfere with their sons' subsequent career choices.

Both parents were dismayed—one can imagine the extent of Ida's dismay especially—when Dwight announced his decision to try for a United States service academy appointment in preparation for a career in the armed services. They made no secret of their wish that he would not. But they did not use his love for them as a weapon against his purpose or raise opposition that might have alienated him from them or the family home. There is a sense in which his choice of a career may be said to represent a triumph of the town's influence over his family's influence upon his mind and character during the years of his growing up.

Abilene, as the northern terminus of the Chisholm Trail and the western terminus of the Kansas Pacific Railroad, had become in the late 1860's and early 1870's the prototype of all Wild Western cow towns. The wild days ended in 1872 when the railroad terminus shifted westward, but the memory of those days was still very much alive in the town in which the Eisenhower sons grew up. It strongly influenced the forms and spirit of children's play (cowboys and Indians was the favorite game among young boys), and it established standards of value and behavior that, if consistent in some respects with those of the Eisenhower religion, were very different from these in total effect. Christian pacifism—the quiet endurance of insult, the turning of the other cheek—was not acceptable, was not even understood, as a general way of conduct on the Western frontier of Indian fighters and buffalo hunters and cattlemen herding across open range.

In the wild frontier tradition, the fist fights between Abilene boys during the 1890's and the early 1900's were of a ferocity almost incredible to later generations of that same town. Often they ended only when one combatant was stretched senseless on the ground. Dwight, when he was just turning thirteen, engaged a boy named Wesley Merrifield in a fight that was prolonged and sanguinary even by Abilene standards. Merrifield was heavier and faster than Dwight, and he gave much more punishment than he received. But Dwight, though brutally beaten, could not be knocked out and refused to quit. Witnesses, vividly remembering the encounter forty years later, swore it lasted more than two hours, long after each boy was too exhausted to strike an effective blow. Finally, according to this remembrance, Merrifield gasped, "I can't lick you, Ike." Whereupon Dwight supposedly replied, through thickly swollen lips, "Well, Wes, I haven't licked you."

Extracurricular activities, chiefly athletic, greatly involved him throughout his high school years. He played well, without starring, on the football and baseball teams—this while earning his own way with long hours of out-of-school labor. Yet his scholastic record was high; it was in fact among the highest in his class, though his schoolmates would recall that he was only an "average" student. When he graduated in 1909 he had a vague desire to con-

TEXT CONTINUED ON PAGE 23

Sartorially splendid for a Kansas boy, Ike posed for the picture above in June, 1911, while stopping in Chicago on his way to West Point, where he shed his civilian clothes for crisp cadet grays.

15

The Kansans

Dwight D. Eisenhower was raised in the middle of the Kansas countryside, a place at once sprawlingly open and forbiddingly bleak, promising of abundance and exacting in demands. It had been the land of buffalo-hunting plainsmen, of Pawnee and Kansas Indians—until the territory was opened up to the white settlers in 1854. First they came in covered wagons, building towns and laying out farms. They quarreled over the morality of owning Negroes, and in 1856, John Brown and his sons butchered some slave holders at Pottawatomie Creek. Brown was called a jayhawker, and Bleeding Kansas was called the Jayhawker State when it came into the Union without slaves in 1861. But the bad feeling raged on through the Civil War, with visits from across the Missouri by Quantrill's raiders—a band that included Cole Younger and Frank and Jesse James. After the war, the railroads cut through the state, and with them came the soldiers and the white buffalo-hunters. They piled bison hides as high as the imposing three-story building in Dodge City; the buffalo nearly died off; and the Indians went hungry and burned out the farmers. The railroads attracted big drives of cattle from Texas. The Chisholm Trail ran straight to the railhead in Abilene, which became America's first cow town, with whiskey, women, hot baths, or all three at once served up in makeshift tents. Abilene got a real shoot-first lawman called Wild Bill Hickok, who had hair down to his shoulders, holsters sewn into his breeches where pockets should have been, and enforced a certain amount of peace and quiet in Abilene. Although it remained a relatively quiet town, it was settled all the same by a hard bunch of sodbusters, railroad men, soldiers, and cattlemen. The Eisenhower boys did not grow up expecting anything to come easily or to be the same as it had been the time before. Kansans learned at an early age to respect achievement, brains, and flexibility.

The excitement caused by the arrival of trains
in Abilene is captured on the opposite page
in a late nineteenth-century sketch by a native
Kansan, Joseph McCoy. At the left,
a freight car of the famed Union Pacific
Railroad speeds past a signal on the Kansas
line. Tracks stretch across the flat countryside
(above) interrupted only by a small hamlet
that has grown up around a railroad junction.

Many of the distinguishing features of Kansas—
a wide, rolling land dotted by small towns—
have changed little since Eisenhower was born.
Above, a typical Kansas main street lies hot
and still under the midday sun. On the opposite
page (top) a new grain elevator and a church
steeple jut above the corn fields; a bin (bottom
left) is filled to the bursting point with the
autumn corn harvest; and Herefords (bottom
right) graze before shipment to the slaughter
houses. At right, sunflowers (the state flower)
grow beside a telephone pole on which the
local candidate for sheriff has nailed a poster
announcing his availability for office.

Now a museum, the restored Eisenhower house in Abilene still has the furniture and decorations collected by Ida Eisenhower. It was in the dining room above that Dwight and his brothers ate their favorite meal, "puddin' meat." On Sundays David gathered his family in the front parlor (right) for the weekly Bible reading. The room held one of Ida Eisenhower's treasures—the ebony piano she bought with part of her dowry.

In an old River Brethren cemetery located
between Hope and Abilene, headstones
(above) mark the graves of three generations
of Eisenhowers. The small farms on which
the early Eisenhowers made their living have
been transformed into large, mechanized
farms run by men with degrees in "agricultural
engineering." At right, an old windmill,
no longer in use and with most of its blades
missing, stands alone on a Kansas plain.

Ike's graduating class at West Point produced fifty-nine officers who attained the rank of general—including two five-star generals; the class of 1915 became known as "the class the stars fell on." One five-star general, Dwight D. Eisenhower, is tenth from left, front row, in the photograph below; the other, Omar N. Bradley, is second from right in the front row.

TEXT CONTINUED FROM PAGE 15

tinue his education, but the desire was far from urgent. He had no notion of where he wished to go to college nor what he wanted his major subject to be.

Then in the summer of 1910, Dwight formed a close friendship with a boy named Everett E. "Swede" Hazlett, Jr., who had obtained an appointment to the United States Naval Academy. He persuaded Dwight to try for such an appointment himself so that the two could be together at Annapolis, and he helped Dwight prepare for the required competitive examination, which he took in October, 1910. Dwight scored 87.5 out of a possible 100 points, but when the appointment came through it was to West Point rather than Annapolis. He then discovered that he was ineligible for the Naval Academy: the regulations required that one enter before his twentieth birthday, and Dwight's was already past.

The young man who emerged from this background to board the eastbound train in June, 1911, did not emerge in bold relief. It would seem that everything conspired to smother such tendencies as he may have had (they were remarkably few, or none) to go to extremes—to *any* extreme. It was symbolically apt that he should have grown up in the precise middle of the country, an area neither north nor south, east nor west, but where all four met and mingled (geographically, culturally, historically) in approximately equal proportions. No situation could have been better designed to produce the all-American boy—sound of body, wholesome of spirit, smiling of disposition, and possessed of a mind not inclined toward probing analysis of world or self, but quick, accurate, and efficient as a tool of practical action.

He seems to have had only one very definite ambition when he signed West Point's official register as Cadet Dwight David Eisenhower: he wanted to star on the Army football team. He had at last managed to star as a tackle on the Abilene High School team in 1910, when he returned for part-time graduate work to help him prepare for academy entrance. He had now achieved his full height of 5 feet 10 1/2 inches; he had put on an increased weight of hard muscle (he weighed 190 pounds). And in the autumn of his second year at the Point, Dwight made a good start toward realizing his ambition. He played halfback on the Army team so well that some sports writers predicted All-American honors for him. Then fate intervened to confirm him in the generally relaxed, unambitious attitudes seemingly most natural to him. A knee twisted in a game with Carlisle (this was the Carlisle team of the immortal Jim Thorpe) was severely injured the following week in a game with Tufts, ending his football career forever.

The disappointment was perhaps the bitterest he ever suffered. His dream of glory lost, he impressed his roommate and closest friend at the Point as one who had "lost interest in life" and was content merely "to exist until graduation shall set him free."

Certainly his over-all West Point record was far from brilliant; few could have augured from it a future greatness. Throughout almost the whole of his cadet career he remained a private in the ranks, with no apparent desire to be anything more; the highest rank he ever attained was that of color sergeant. In his 1915 graduating class of 164 he stood ninety-fifth in conduct. He was in the

Mamie Doud, at left, was an ebullient eighteen-year-old when she met fledgling Lieutenant Eisenhower in San Antonio, his first military post after graduation from West Point. Below are Mamie and Ike just after their marriage in 1916.

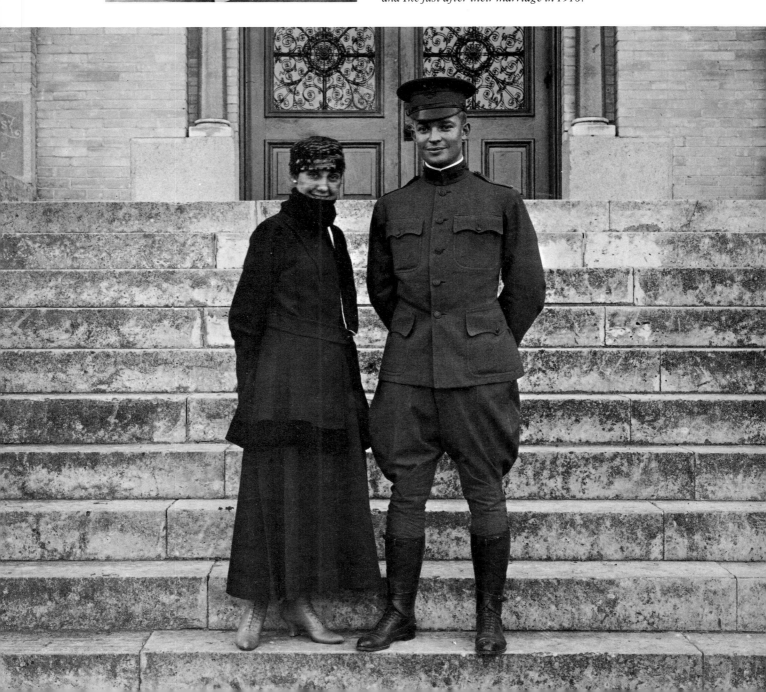

upper third of his class in scholarship for the four years, but at the very bottom of the upper third. His graduation order was sixty-one. He was, however, "generally liked and admired" by teachers and fellow cadets, as Swede Hazlett discovered when he visited the Point a few days before graduation ceremonies. The absence from Dwight of success anxiety, his apparent total lack of any desire to dazzle or overawe, contributed to his popularity.

Not that he was indifferent to, or unaware of, the impression he made on others. He wanted to please people, he had a happy faculty for making others want to please him, with the result that those in a position to advance him were almost invariably predisposed in his favor. Nor was he lacking in the ability to work hard to fulfill specific assignments or, on occasion, work toward definite goals of his own choosing.

He demonstrated this in his courtship of a slender, dark-haired, violet-eyed girl of eighteen whom he first met in early October, 1915, just two weeks after he had reported for duty on his first Army assignment as a second lieutenant in the 19th Infantry at Fort Sam Houston in San Antonio, Texas. The girl's name was Mamie Geneva Doud. The daughter of a prosperous Denver family whose fortune had come from meat packing in the Middle West, she was accustomed to a life of ease and luxury such as Dwight Eisenhower, as a child, could not have imagined possible for himself. She was pretty, vivacious, funloving, popular, and not at all eager to marry—not for years and years. She did nothing initially to encourage Lieutenant Eisenhower's suit; she did a good deal to discourage it. But he was determined to marry her, and his pursuit of her was as skillful as it was indefatigable (he was clever enough to court her family's favor as a major element of her own). On St. Valentine's Day of 1916 she accepted his West Point class ring. Five months later, on July 1, 1916, they were married in the Doud house at 750 Lafayette Street in Denver. On that same day he was promoted to first lieutenant.

At that time, of course, all Army professionals saw their immediate futures in the lurid light of the great war that had been raging in Europe since August, 1914. Young Lieutenant Eisenhower, recognizing the need to employ new weapons and tactics if the bloody stalemate of trench warfare on the Western Front was to be broken, early fastened his attention upon the two weapons that might achieve this purpose, namely, the tank and the airplane. It was the latter that first intrigued him—so much that in early 1917 he considered requesting a transfer from the infantry to the air corps. Mamie tearfully opposed this plan, which she considered suicidal, and when he learned she was pregnant he heeded her pleas.

After the United States entered the war in April, 1917, he yearned to go overseas—his chance for future high command seemed to depend upon his acquiring battle experience—but he proved so effective an instructor and trainer of men that he was given a succession of such assignments. The last of them stemmed from his continuing interest in tanks: he was ordered to take command of Camp Colt, a tank training center at Gettysburg, Pennsylvania. This was on March 24, 1918. He had then been a father precisely six months; for on September 24, 1917, Mamie had given

John Sheldon Doud, Ike's second son, above with Mamie, was born in 1922. Their first son died the year before.

OVERLEAF: *A much-decorated Chief of Staff, General MacArthur, and a subordinate, Major Eisenhower, stand at ease after disbanding the Bonus March in 1932.*

birth to their first child, a son whom they named Doud Dwight.

The Camp Colt assignment was a remarkably responsible one for a twenty-seven-year-old captain. (He had been promoted to this permanent rank in mid-May, 1917.) It was also remarkably difficult. He had no tanks with which to train and indeed no adequate facilities at the outset for sheltering and feeding the thousands of men who began to pour into his command. Yet he succeeded brilliantly. "While Commanding Officer of the Tank Corps Training Center," said his citation for the Distinguished Service Medal ultimately awarded him, "he displayed unusual zeal, foresight, and marked administrative ability in the organization, training, and preparation for overseas service of technical troops of the Tank Corps." He never achieved his ambition to command a tank outfit in battle; the embarkation orders he finally received were canceled by the armistice.

There followed for him, as for other American professional soldiers, a period of letdown and seemingly meaningless drift through a series of routine assignments. For Eisenhower, more than most of his West Point classmates, the chance for any great future distinction seemed slight indeed. He had achieved the temporary rank of lieutenant colonel at Camp Colt (the promotion was dated October 14, 1918, his twenty-eighth birthday) when he had six thousand men under his command. He still held this rank a year later when he sought, and for some reason was refused, permission to enter the Infantry School. This was a severe blow to such career hopes as he had, since graduation from a service school was generally required for entrance into the Command and General Staff School at Fort Leavenworth, and graduation from the latter was generally a prerequisite for promotion to high command. He reverted to his permanent rank of captain on June 30, 1920. Three days later he was promoted to the permanent rank of major, but that was the highest rank he seemed likely to attain in a shrunken peacetime army for as far as he could see into the future. Then came personal tragedy: in January, 1921, the Eisenhowers' three-year-old son, whom they called Icky, died of scarlet fever.

There were times during the next few years when watching the prospering careers of his five brothers while his own languished, Dwight Eisenhower considered resigning his commission. He might have done so if a sufficiently attractive offer had come to him from business or if he had not come under the tutelage and influence of Brigadier General Fox Conner, an outstanding officer under whom he served as executive officer in the Panama Canal Zone from 1922 to 1924. (From Panama in the summer of 1922, Mamie returned to Denver where, on August 3, she gave birth to a second son, named John Sheldon Doud Eisenhower.)

Conner was convinced that a second world war was coming and that Eisenhower, along with a certain Major George C. Marshall, of whom Eisenhower then heard for the first time, was destined to play an important role in it. He stimulated Eisenhower to study and work hard in preparation. He was largely instrumental in securing Eisenhower's entrance into the Command and General Staff School in August, 1925, despite the major's handicap of not having gone through his service school. And he felt justified in the

judgment he had formed of his protégé when Eisenhower graduated first from the school in a class of some 275, including a number of the best brains in the Army, after months of competitive mental strains so intense that many an officer broke under them. This, along with the "S" (for "superior") that he annually received on his efficiency rating, meant that he would be placed high on the General Staff Corps Eligible List.

Six months later, while serving as executive officer for the 24th Infantry at Fort Benning, Georgia, he was asked if he would accept assignment to the American Battle Monuments Commission to prepare a guidebook to the European battlefields on which Americans had fought in 1917–18. Few professional soldiers could have seen such an invitation as a beckoning of opportunity. It presented itself as a dull, grinding job, big with difficulties and minuscule in possible rewards. But the work would be done under the appraising eye of the chairman of the commission, who was none other than General John J. Pershing, and if the job was done well it would earn for its doer the gratitude and admiration of America's first soldier—a value difficult to measure but certainly very real. Eisenhower accepted the assignment. He spent six hard months on it in Washington, where he was aided by suggestions from his youngest brother, Milton, who had majored in industrial journalism at Kansas State College and who was now assistant to the Secretary of Agriculture. The result was a guidebook that still remains among the most useful of reference works on World War I. Pershing was appreciative. In a letter to Major General Robert H. Allen, Chief of Infantry, written on the day Eisenhower's commission detail expired (August 15, 1927), Pershing spoke of the "splendid service" that the major "has rendered since being with us." Pershing went on: "In the discharge of his duties, which were most difficult, and which were rendered even more difficult by reason of the short time available for their completion, he has shown superior ability not only in visualizing his work as a whole but in executing its many details in an efficient and timely manner. What he has done was accomplished only by the exercise of unusual intelligence and constant devotion to duty."

Eisenhower remained in Washington for another year. He entered the Army War College in September, 1927, graduating from it in June, 1928, and then accepted another detail to the American Battle Monuments Commission to prepare a new edition of his guidebook. He was sent to France for this purpose and remained there, headquartered in Paris, from midsummer of 1928 to September of 1929. During that year he evidently lost some of that sense of urgency that Fox Conner's dire predictions had aroused in him. How could one see impending world war in a Europe and an America that happily basked in the warm light of economic prosperity and, with much-publicized ceremony, signed international pacts renouncing war forever as an instrument of national policy?

But all this changed abruptly, drastically, a few weeks after the Eisenhowers had returned to the United States. The stock market collapsed, heralding two decades of tragic turmoil for the whole civilized world. Soon, increasing millions of increasingly desperate unemployed walked the streets of Europe, America, the

Far East. There followed political repercussions of grave import: the rise of Japanese militarism, leading to aggressive war against China; the ruthless conquest of Ethiopia by Mussolini's Italy; Hitler's Nazi conquest of power in Germany, leading to the forcible annexation of Austria and the rape of the Sudetenland from Czechoslovakia with the passive aid of Chamberlain's Britain and Daladier's France; the Spanish Civil War in which Fascist Franco was openly aided by Hitler and Mussolini. With each passing year, the dark signs and portents accumulated. Now, none could deny the increasing possibility of a second world war, and no longer was the professional soldier a superfluous, even a slightly ridiculous, element of American society, as he had been to much of the general public throughout the 1920's.

During the first half of the Depression decade, Eisenhower was stationed in Washington, first in the office of the Assistant Secretary of War, then in the office of the United States Army Chief of Staff, General Douglas MacArthur. When MacArthur, on detached service from the Army, accepted the post of military adviser to the Philippine Commonwealth, Eisenhower accompanied him to Manila at his request as his chief assistant. Four years later, when World War II began with Hitler's attack on Poland, Major Eisenhower was still on detached service in the Philippines. He returned to the United States in December, 1939.

Sixteen months later he at last achieved what had been, throughout most of his career, his ultimate ambition. On March 11, 1941, having been elevated from the post of Executive Officer of the 15th Infantry Division to that of Chief of Staff for the Ninth Army Corps in Fort Lewis, Washington, he was appointed to the rank of full colonel (temporary). Great was the jubilation in the Eisenhower home; both John and Mamie would remember that no promotion he received afterward pleased him as greatly as this. His joy was unalloyed—until fellow officers on the post, congratulating him, predicted that the "chickens" on his shoulders would soon be replaced by a general's stars. "Damn it," he grumbled to his son, "as soon as you get a promotion they start talking about another one. Why can't they let a guy be happy with what he has? They take all the joy out of it." Nevertheless, he could not help but have known that the prophecy made by his colleagues was of very probable truth. Dire circumstances favored it.

From the moment of his return from the Philippines, where his job had been to help the commonwealth prepare her defenses against an aggressive Japan, Eisenhower had expressed to all and sundry his conviction that the United States would soon be at war. He had become known to his fellow officers in the 15th Infantry as Alarmist Ike during the period of "phony war" when, through the winter of 1939–40, all was quiet on the Western Front. But the alarm he had then expressed abruptly ceased to be at all remarkable in the spring of 1940. The German conquest of Norway, Denmark, the Low Countries, and France in swift succession, the imminent threat of a German conquest of a Britain standing alone under continuous air attack—these forced a reluctant America to institute her first peacetime military conscription, coupled with an accelerated program of voluntary enlistments. An army of 172,000

After his return from the Philippines,
Ike was posted to Fort Ord, California,
as an executive officer for the 15th
Infantry Division. A mess line at the fort
is depicted in the painting above by
Barse Miller. During the huge Louisiana
maneuvers in 1941, Colonel Eisenhower
served as Chief of Staff for the Third Army.
In this capacity, Ike conceived and
directed much of the strategy that won the
victory for the Third Army. He observes
troop maneuvers through field glasses, above
left. At left, Eisenhower confers with
Lieutenant Colonel James L. Bradley.

was being expanded into one of 1,500,000. And on the very day that Eisenhower made "chicken" colonel, President Roosevelt signed into law the Lend-Lease Bill, which committed the United States irrevocably to a British victory.

The commitment could not be fulfilled by material aid alone, especially in view of the ominous situation in the Far East. America must fight; all her industrial, naval, and military might must be mobilized and made effective on the battlefield. This was made abundantly clear through the spring and summer of 1941 by stupendous events in the Mediterranean area, climaxed by the German invasion of Russia in late June. Again, German forces seemed invincible; most American military experts were of the opinion that European Russia would be a German conquest before full winter came. Simultaneously there was a deepening of the crisis in the Far East, where Japan moved into French Indochina with Vichy France's permission, clearly presaging further aggressive moves to the south, where vital U. S. interests were at stake.

The over-all American response to these accumulating threats seemed to most knowledgeable observers woefully inadequate. The White House made public gestures expressive of utmost determination. But industrial mobilization lagged. So did the Army training program. The Army lacked vehicles and weapons with which to train, there were grave deficiencies in small-unit command, and there was an acute shortage of capable general officers.

To remedy these deficiencies, or take needed steps toward doing so, General George C. Marshall, Army Chief of Staff, with his high-command associates, laid plans that summer for the largest peacetime military maneuvers in American history. They were plans that involved Colonel Eisenhower. He was named Chief of Staff for Lieutenant General Walter Krueger's Third Army, which, as the "Blue" force, engaged Lieutenant General Ben Lear's Second Army, the "Red" force, in a mock battle fought in two phases across a storm-swept Louisiana in late September. The Blues won decisive victories in both phases, and for this, Eisenhower's staff work was deemed in large part responsible. For the first time in his career he was mentioned by name in national press service dispatches and in one syndicated column. "Colonel Eisenhower... who conceived and directed the strategy that routed the Second Army," reported Drew Pearson and Robert S. Allen, "has a steel-trap mind plus unusual physical vigor [and] to him the military profession is a science, and he began watching and studying the German Army five years ago."

He was promptly promoted to the rank of brigadier general (temporary). He remained as the Third Army's Chief of Staff, stationed at Fort Sam Houston, San Antonio, Texas, through the weeks of mounting Far Eastern crisis that followed.

On the morning of the first Sunday in December, despite a week of fourteen-hour days that had left him "dead tired," as he confessed to Mamie, he arose early and went to his office. He worked until noon, then went home to nap, leaving instructions that he be phoned if anything of importance came up. He had been asleep for an hour when the phone beside his bed awoke him. The Japanese, he was told, were attacking Pearl Harbor.

Flames engulf the fleet anchored at Pearl Harbor (above) just after the Japanese attack on December 7, 1941.

Ten-year-old Dwight, at left above, poses for a family portrait with his mother and father and five brothers. Roy is at center, between his parents; the others, from left to right, are Edgar, Earl, Milton, and Arthur.

Abilene Remembered

by MILTON S. EISENHOWER

The following account is from a conversation with Dr. Milton S. Eisenhower, youngest of the Eisenhower brothers. Dr. Eisenhower, lawyer, educator, and President of the Johns Hopkins University from 1956 to 1966, remembers life in Abilene, and in the Eisenhower family, at the turn of the century.

It was a quiet, law-abiding place. Everyone was putting something in: the town was putting in paved streets, Dad was wiring our house, I was able to equip our home with a serviceable gas water-heater. When the first automobile came rolling into town (a White steamer, as I recall), everyone stopped to look and make comments on its impracticality.

There was little evidence of Abilene's former frontier character—cattle driving, drinking, and shooting—though all of these were a part of the local stories we delighted to hear. The stories had long since lost whatever accuracy they may have once possessed. Remember that my grandfather brought his family from Pennsylvania in 1878, and my mother came from Virginia to join a brother at Topeka at about the same time. We boys were two full generations removed from the frontier dramatized in modern Westerns. The earliest excitement I personally recollect was the flood of 1903. There was, nevertheless, a residuum of the pioneer spirit in the town's unsophisticated atmosphere, its ingrained friendliness, and its isolation from the rest of the world.

The isolation was political and economic as well as just a prevailing state of mind. Politically, I can't remember anything earth shaking happening at all, anything that threatened the firm control that the Republican party had exercised on the region ever since Kansas' stormy Civil War days. People still talked about the visit William McKinley made to Abilene before I was born: the three elder Eisenhower brothers led the parade, carrying torches. Economically, of course, the town had advanced far beyond those early days when, as Dad expressed it, the main problem was "how to trade eggs for sugar and salt." But, beyond the shipment of grain by rail out to the East, there was very little outside contact. Self-sufficiency, personal initiative, and responsibility were prized; radicalism was unheard of. So it's little wonder we boys grew up to be moderates and conservatives—in short, Republicans.

Socially, things were a bit more complicated, or so my brother Edgar felt. He has contended that Abilene was split by tracks running east and west, and that although there were many crossings, some of them were too difficult to make. On the north side were the more affluent residential areas of the town; south of the tracks were lovely but more modest dwellings—and the Eisenhowers. The elementary school we all went to was right across the street from our house, but the seventh and eighth grades were in a building on the north side, the Garfield School. Making that transition was a real challenge for several of my older brothers. Edgar and especially Ike each got involved in a whale of a fight when they made the change, fights that became as much a part of the Abilene story as anything that Wild Bill Hickok had done. But by the time Earl and I came along, all was serene and uneventful. Perhaps Ike had settled the issue for all time.

I honestly don't remember the rivalry with the north side

boys that Edgar has spoken and written about. One reason for this may be that Edgar often had the job of taking the surplus vegetables we grew in our garden across the tracks in a wagon and selling them to the "snooty" families of his schoolmates. My regular after-school job—working in the drug store—was free of any such hostility. And I don't think that Ike, who pulled ice at the creamery, ran into much of it there either. In addition to jobs like these, which we took in order to bring in extra cash for the family, there were numerous chores that had to be done. The garden had to be hoed, the orchard tended to, the cow barn cleaned, or the horses rubbed down. Of all these regularly rotated chores, the least desirable by far was getting up at 5 A.M. to light the stoves. But there never seemed to be a lack of time for our big meals or for family fun: the rule was that after you had done your lessons, your chores, and your work, all your free time was your own.

Some of the free time, of course, was taken up with going to church, or with Bible readings. We all went to the River Brethren Sunday School, and Grandfather, who was a minister of the Brethren and who lived with us, never seemed to lose his ministerial aspect. His black beard and black tie were the trademarks of his calling. It is striking that in the earliest group picture of our family (1902), Father, a man of the new century, wears no beard—just a small mustache—and no tie.

Mother had been raised as a Lutheran, but at the time I can remember best she had become interested in the Bible students of the Watchtower Society. It was she who organized the meetings that used to fill our living room on Sundays. And it was she, with her consistently biblical approach to life (when she was a little girl back in Virginia, she won a prize for memorizing 1,675 verses of the Bible in six months), who saw to it that religion would be just as much a part of our home life as eating or sleeping.

Dad's devotion to the Bible may have been less doctrinaire, more intellectual, than Mother's: he kept a Greek edition by his bedside for checking questions of interpretation or punctuation. But his pacifism, though less outspoken than hers, was no less heartfelt. That old religious abhorrence of war—who can say now that it was naïve?—was in some ways a troublesome conviction. As World War I developed, everyone in town was down on pacifists and all things German. At one point, even though several of her sons were in uniform, Mother was in real danger of being arrested because of her articulate pacifism and her German-sounding name. It was only the intervention of an influential friend that kept her out of jail. Ironically, in World War II, I was given the loathsome job of resettling the Japanese-Americans on the West Coast (there was then no anti-German sentiment whatsoever), but I found I had a terrific struggle with people who wanted to treat these citizens with the senseless severity that had been directed toward persons of German descent in 1917.

There must have been a real conflict in Mother's heart when Ike got his appointment to West Point. Neither she nor Dad took any part in helping him make that decision. And with the rest of us, their hands-off policy was the same, perhaps because Dad continued to feel strongly that Grandfather had made a mistake in trying so hard to get him to be a farmer. The only exception that I recall to this policy was the openly expressed hope that Edgar might be a doctor (as it turned out, he wanted to become a lawyer, and did so). Ike, on the other hand, at that time was not sure of what he wanted to do. He had been in everything at school (on teams, in societies, etc.), and through it all he was a good student. I think he was confident that the right thing would turn up. And of course it did: when Swede Hazlett came home from Annapolis, his accounts of life and education at the academy made a big impression on Ike and succeeded in interesting him in Annapolis and West Point. Knowing that he was a good student and had friends to back him up (particularly the editors of the town's two newspapers), Ike was reasonably confident of his chances. And what motivated him to try for Annapolis or West Point was doubtless the prospect of getting a good education free—that was surely as important as the idea of a military career. Ultimately I believe it was the age factor (at the last moment he learned he was too old to enter Annapolis) that made him decide to go to West Point.

The idyllic, withdrawn character of Abilene changed, of course, as World War I developed—just as the careers of the Eisenhower brothers branched out then from their home town. Without saying so we all apparently shared the belief that "If you stay home you will always be looked upon as a boy." I happened to be home when Ike left to get the train East in 1911; Mother seemed perfectly composed, but after he left she cried.

It wasn't because of her pacifism, however, that Mother seemed rather indifferent toward the success of Dwight as a professional soldier. She simply had her own standards, and they were different. She did not consider success to be related to rank or position or income; a great man was considerate and good—this was the sole criterion. Indeed, when asked after World War II whether she wasn't enormously proud of her famous son, she replied, "Which one?" This was not a clever response; it was wholly harmonious with her philosophy. Another anecdote along these lines is that during the war a traveling lady from New York went out of her way (she was San Francisco bound) to go to Abilene and meet Mother. When Mother gathered that the lady had a son in uniform she exclaimed, "Why, you know, I have a son in the Army in Europe, too!"

In family reunions spread over the past two decades, we

brothers have talked much of our early, gay, and satisfying life in Abilene. On one thing we are agreed: the total environment and certainly the simple rules in our home taught us as youngsters to be self-reliant, independent, and responsible. I have often felt, and I suppose I still do, that urbanization, with its congestion of living, its lack of truly responsible things for youngsters to do, is less conducive to stimulating the development of these qualities than is life in a community like Abilene. Thomas Jefferson, in the late 1790's, argued that democracy was nurtured in, and wedded to, the rural areas. However, he lived long enough to see the beginnings of urbanization and specialization in working; so he then argued that we could keep democracy only so long as there was a rising level of education and understanding among *all* the people, for only then would the mass judgment by those who hold the basic social power possibly be valid.

Growing Up

by EDGAR EISENHOWER

Edgar Eisenhower, second eldest of the Eisenhower brothers, is currently practicing law in Tacoma, Washington. In 1960, Wood & Reber, Inc. brought out his memoirs, Six Roads From Abilene.* *These reminiscences are taken from passages of that book.*

. . . it was not until [Dwight] was elected to the Presidency that the entire family was pulled into the limelight. The full realization that life never again would be quite the same for us was driven home to me as I stood with the family watching Dwight take the oath of office at the inauguration ceremonies in 1953. The pageantry and solemnity of the occasion would be impressive to any American, but it certainly touched us deeper. There was our brother, Dwight David Eisenhower, taking the same oath that George Washington and Abraham Lincoln had intoned. He was standing there, a figure that would be secure in the history books for all time. Generations of school children would be reading about Dwight Eisenhower two hundred years from now. It was an eerie and solemn feeling.

I doubt if ever I shall be so deeply stirred again. The Presidency had become something near and personal. I was remembering Dwight at that moment only as my kid brother, the tyke I had once shared a bed with, back in Abilene; the

scrappy little guy I had battled all through boyhood. . . .

Our lives as youngsters were full and purposeful. There was plenty of fun and good old-fashioned pranks. We played games that kept us happy and exuberant. But behind all of this activity was a stern daily routine of constant discipline and the solid exposure to the principles of life and the values that were planted and developed in our minds.

Mother, I am sure, was proud of her sons. There were times, of course, when we were noisy and a little too enthusiastically original, but still we were healthy and faithful and good natured. Each of us had individual complexities, needing pulling or pushing occasionally, but Mother always seemed to know what to say and what to do to straighten us out. . . .

To help meet household expenses, Mother often sent Dwight and me over to the north side of town with our little red wagon loaded with sweet corn, peas, beans, tomatoes, and eggs. We concentrated on those who never had gardens of their own. Knocking on all those doors distressed me. I didn't like the attitude of the customers, nor the way they fingered

our vegetables, taking only the nice ones and paying us only a slim price. Some of them even made nasty remarks about our produce, even though I knew our stuff was as good as could be found in town. I resented this. It admittedly made me feel a bit inferior. I suppose this is the reason I always felt that the railroad tracks separated Abilene into two classes—those who

* Six Roads From Abilene BY JOHN MCCALLUM © 1960 WOOD & REBER, INC.

lived north of the tracks were, in my mind, a little bit better than those who lived south of the tracks. Being a little older than Dwight, I was perhaps more sensitive than he was about this, because I mentioned my feeling to him many years later and he said he never had any such feeling. I never outgrew it, however. I have since realized that you must take a lot of abuse in life while you are working your way up, but I also feel anyone who is making an honest effort to better himself is entitled to some respect. . . .

There are just so many hours to a waking day, even if every minute of them is occupied attending school, working at odd jobs, or playing on some athletic team. But all of us found time to participate in the cross-town encounters.

This wrangling persisted only after we transferred to the intermediate school over on the north side of town. You see, there were only six grades at the south side school where we first attended, so we had to go to the north side for the seventh and eighth grades and for high school. The north side kids resented our coming to their school. So there were fights. We didn't go around looking for them, but we never ran from fights either.

These fist-fights between the best fighters from the north and south sides of Abilene were never actually planned affairs. No one knew in advance who the combatants would be. They just happened. Something would boil up in a game, or while marching into school, and the next thing we knew a battle was on. If it was a real good scrap, that settled everything between north and south, and we were accepted.

On one occasion I got involved in one of those scuffles, and another time Dwight battled for our honor. Both fights were real grim battles. Dwight's scrap happened about a year after mine.

He was about fifteen years old and smaller and more slender than he was when he went out for football at West Point. His match paralleled mine in some respects. His opponent was much bigger, and older, too; a heavy-set, thick-necked boy named Wes Merrifield. Dwight seemed to be over-matched. To look at them together on the street you would have thought that Wes would have killed him. But my brother could take a punch, and he could deliver one. He wasn't too fast, but he had our dad's fighting heart and stubbornness, and he refused to go down easily. . . .

It was toe to toe slugging for nearly two hours, neither boy admitting defeat or giving quarter. Finally when their strength was gone, both boys realized it was useless to go on. . . .

A lot of the kids who hadn't given Dwight much of a chance rushed up to him and slapped him on the back. To them, he was a hero, but he didn't feel like one. To me, the fight showed Dwight's dogged determination and tenacity. These are traits that have stuck with him through the years and have helped him over many a hurdle when things looked black. . . .

During our senior year in high school Dwight and I had talked about going to college. We knew we were too poor for our parents to help both of us at the same time. So we decided that I, being the older, would first go to college one year. Dwight would work and give me his earnings and then I would stay out of school the next year, work, and give my earnings to Dwight. We planned to alternate in school this way until both of us were graduated. It would take eight years to finish the four-year course, but we were willing.

So off to Michigan I went. In my first year I enrolled in the Literary School. Dwight, true to his word, got a job and sent me $200 of his salary. Now that I think about it, I never did pay him back the loan, and he never asked for it. But it set a pattern for the family. We have always helped each other from that time on. I have paid more than the $200 to other members of the family. . . .

Incidentally, Dwight stopped off at Ann Arbor to visit with me on his way to the Point. This was to be the last time for fifteen years that we were able to get together. The next time I saw him was in 1926 when our family held a reunion at Abilene.

Our oldest brother, Arthur, was the first of the Eisenhower sons to achieve material success. While Dwight was at West Point and I was at Michigan, Arthur set a pattern for the rest of us to follow by getting a job as a messenger in a Kansas City bank and working his way up. He was just getting established in banking while Dwight and I were in school. To help meet living expenses, Arthur got himself a roommate. . . . It was Harry S. Truman! . . .

Though we have always had a lot of affection for one another, people have asked me, "Ed, hasn't there ever been any envy or jealousy among you brothers?"

"Heck, no," I reply, honestly. "As a matter of fact, we are probably mentally boosting one another all the time."

Personally, it has never occurred to me to be the slightest bit envious about any of the successes of my brothers. I know they feel the same way. Why on earth should anybody be jealous of a member of his own family? I think a person should be proud of anything one of his brothers contributes toward the good of mankind. Dwight, of course, has done far more than any of the rest of us for his country, but we have all tried to be contributing Americans.

*Hitler's blitzkrieg moves with cruel speed
through Yugoslavia, below, in April, 1941, leaving
a wake of burning, devastated villages.*

II

A COMMANDER
FOR THE CRUSADE

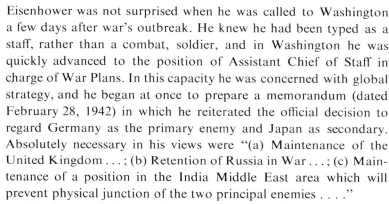

Eisenhower was not surprised when he was called to Washington a few days after war's outbreak. He knew he had been typed as a staff, rather than a combat, soldier, and in Washington he was quickly advanced to the position of Assistant Chief of Staff in charge of War Plans. In this capacity he was concerned with global strategy, and he began at once to prepare a memorandum (dated February 28, 1942) in which he reiterated the official decision to regard Germany as the primary enemy and Japan as secondary. Absolutely necessary in his views were "(a) Maintenance of the United Kingdom . . . ; (b) Retention of Russia in War . . . ; (c) Maintenance of a position in the India Middle East area which will prevent physical junction of the two principal enemies . . . ."

Of these strategic necessities, the most pressing at the moment seemed to be the second. Russia had survived the first German onslaught, as few American military professionals had believed she could, but she had been grievously injured and remained in the gravest of danger. Could she stand against the massive offensive that must inevitably be renewed in the coming spring and summer? She might not, Eisenhower indicated, unless there was "immediate and definite action" to aid her, partly through increased lend-lease but chiefly "through the early initiation of operations that will draw off from the Russian front sizable portions of the German army, both air and ground." He proposed that the United States devise "at once," in conjunction with the British, a detailed plan of operations against northwest Europe that "from the middle of May onward" would engage "an increasing portion of the German air force and by late summer an increasing amount of his ground forces." In other words, he favored launching a cross-Channel invasion of the Continent in the autumn of 1942.

This, he quickly learned, was out of the question. The British were adamantly opposed to it; they bolstered their opposition with facts. There could not possibly be enough ships and landing craft to make such an operation feasible before the spring of 1943 at the earliest, even if a sufficient number of well-trained troops were available before then, as they were not likely to be. Hence, this Eisenhower proposal, though it perfectly expressed what its author knew to be the Chief of Staff's desire, underwent much revision be-

fore it was presented in a memorandum to the President and the Secretary of War by General Marshall on April 1, 1942. The Marshall Memorandum, as it was called, proposed that all plans and operations be directed toward the "single end" of "an attack, by combined forces of approximately 5,800 combat airplanes and 48 divisions against Western Europe as soon as the necessary means can be accumulated in England." There would be such "means," it was estimated, by April 1, 1943, which became the target date for the cross-Channel operation. In the meantime, preparations were to be made for a limited attack to be launched in September of 1942 if this was necessary to prevent a Russian collapse.

President Roosevelt, approving the proposal on the day he received it, immediately sent his special assistant, Harry Hopkins, to London with Marshall to obtain the concurrence of Prime Minister Winston Churchill and the British chiefs of staff. The two returned to Washington in mid-April convinced (at least, Marshall was convinced) that the British did concur, that they were as firmly committed as the American high command to an invasion of Europe in the spring of 1943. Eisenhower received this news with joy: ". . . at long last . . . we are all definitely committed to one concept of fighting!" he wrote on his desk pad.

But in this he and Marshall were mistaken. What Marshall regarded as an ironclad operational agreement was regarded by the British as a provisional one—an agreement "in principle" whose actual implementation, or lack of it, depended upon contingencies impossible to foresee.

By this time there was a considerable difference between British and American estimates of Russia's ability to withstand German pressure, hence of the amount of Allied aid required to sustain her. The British were in general much more sanguine about Russia's survival capacity than the Americans were; Britain was proportionately less willing to cancel or reduce other operations in order to concentrate on the one that would most immediately succor the Russians. Equally great was the discrepancy between British and American estimates of the scale on which a cross-Channel operation must be launched if it were not to end in disaster.

Indeed, when British estimates of the necessary scale of the invasion (700,000 men the first week) became known to Marshall during the weeks following his London visit, he began to suspect that the figure was deliberately inflated to prevent the operation's timely execution and perhaps prevent its being launched at all. The suspicion was encouraged by Churchill's reiterated proposal, that spring of 1942, to invade North Africa in early autumn, though this would destroy altogether the possibility of any cross-Channel operation at all that year—even the most limited—and would greatly weaken, if not destroy, the chances for a major invasion in 1943. The Americans wondered whether secret political motives underlay the proposal. Was the British Government now working in typically devious ways (the perfidy of "Perfidious Albion" was a basic conviction of some of Marshall's colleagues) to insure that when the war ended, Soviet Russia would be too weak to fill the power vacuum left in Central Europe by the collapse of Hitler and Mussolini? This would at least explain the calm with which the

Hitler, told of Marshal Pétain's request for an armistice, stamps his foot in joy over his conquest of France. England, fighting on alone, was soon subjected to the assaults of the Luftwaffe. England's Coventry Cathedral (opposite) was reduced to rubble in one night.

British seemed to view Russia's agony. It would explain, too, Britain's evident willingness to fight a long-drawn-out war, her evident reluctance to concentrate for the earliest possible decisive blow. And it was not at all in accord with the Roosevelt administration's attitude toward Russia or with the ideas for future world organization that were being developed in the State Department. Thus, behind the smiling façade that the Anglo-American alliance presented to the eyes of the world, disagreement grew into an angry conflict of views during the seven months following Pearl Harbor. The central character of the drama was George Marshall.

In 1942 Marshall was sixty-one years old, but he appeared little older than Eisenhower, who was ten years his junior. Sandy-haired rather than gray, erect and vigorous of body, alert of mind, and with a capacity for long-sustained, concentrated work, he impressed all who dealt with him as a man utterly selfless in his devotion to duty, wholly committed to a high and difficult code of honor. In physique, interest, and mental quality there were a number of similarities between him and Eisenhower. Both were by nature impatient, with fiery tempers whose mastery had been difficult for them. Both had rather bleak, prosaic minds concerned with facts, impatient of all that was fluid, vague, and indefinite.

And out of Marshall's abhorrence of all that seemed to him devious and underhanded, the most dangerous quarrel of the war between the two allies erupted in the summer of 1942. On July 8, Washington was abruptly informed that the British War Cabinet had decided to cancel all preparations for the limited Continental invasion. Instead it proposed the invasion of North Africa in early fall. Marshall's reaction was explosive. He regarded the British action as a violation of the April agreement, a breach of faith that canceled not only the tentative autumn operation against the Continent but the major invasion definitely scheduled for the following spring. There would simply not be enough resources within the next twelve months for both the African *and* French invasions. In his anger, Marshall made a counterproposal, namely, that a virtual ultimatum be presented to the British: either they adhere to the earlier agreement or the United States would shift her major war effort from the Atlantic to the Pacific, assuming a defensive attitude against Germany, except for air operations, and using all available means to "strike decisively against Japan."

Fortunately for the free world, Roosevelt refused to endorse the proposal. Moreover, Roosevelt's refusal stemmed in part from Marshall's own earlier actions. No man had insisted more effectively than Marshall that cooperation between Britain and America was not enough, that there must be an actual unity of the war effort of the two powers. It was he who had forced upon an initially reluctant Roosevelt and Churchill an organizational amalgamation of the supreme British and American military and naval commands in a combined chiefs of staff—an unprecedented international military executive committee. The President, rejecting the alliance-wrecking tactic of ultimatum that Marshall proposed, sent him once again to London with Admiral Ernest King and Harry Hopkins under orders not to insist adamantly upon the reinstatement of every element of the April agreement, but instead to arrive

Blindfolded, Secretary of War Henry L. Stimson, on October 29, 1940, draws the first of the numbers to determine the order in which men will be drafted into the American Army.

General George C. Marshall, at right, chats with Eisenhower. Marshall appointed Ike Commander of the European Theater in 1942.

"at total agreement within one week" on some operation that would engage U.S. ground troops against the Germans in 1942. Consideration must be given North Africa as a possible theater for such an engagement, Roosevelt said.

Marshall had an opportunity on this trip to London to review personally the U.S. command arrangement he had set up there. In late June, he had established a European Theater of Operations, United States Army (ETOUSA). To its command he had assigned Major General Dwight D. Eisenhower.

Marshall, watching closely the work and personal character of his War Plans chief that spring, had of course recognized the similarities between himself and Eisenhower. Because they "thought alike" and "felt alike," it was easy for the two men to work closely together. But there were also differences between them. These, too, Marshall had sensed that spring; they were perhaps as important as the similarities in determining his decision to send Eisenhower to Europe.

Eisenhower was a warmer and more personally likable man than Marshall was; he was far more concerned to be liked than Marshall was. People immensely respected and admired the Chief of Staff, but they did so from a certain distance, which he himself maintained. Eisenhower, on the other hand, was "Ike" to all he met, almost from the moment he met them, and in the radiance of his wide, sunny, lopsided grin, the iciest of natures soon thawed. Joined to this likableness was a sensitiveness to the moods and attitudes of others that made him a near-perfect chairman of meetings where a consensus had to be established. He made people *want* to agree. And finally, as part and parcel of his other-mindedness, Eisenhower's was a far more flexible character, fundamentally, than Marshall's; he could adapt or accommodate himself to a far wider range of situations and points of view than Marshall either could or was willing to try to do.

All this suggested a wise division of over-all function between Marshall and Eisenhower in the Allied war effort as a whole. Marshall's position as the acknowledged leader of the American Joint Chiefs of Staff required him to help determine and then advocate as strongly as possible, within the framework of the Combined Chiefs of Staff, the U.S. position in all matters of controversy between his country and Britain. He must do so at the risk of personally antagonizing his British colleagues. But the task of an American commander of Allied forces in Europe (and it was only realistic to suppose that the commander would be American) was different. He would have to forge and wield the instrument of Allied policy, and to this end he must never permit differences between himself and his allies to grow into actual antagonisms. As long as he was firmly ordered and firmly sustained by his superiors, his most important qualities would be precisely those that Eisenhower possessed in greatest abundance—tact, good humor, a genius for creative compromise.

If Marshall had not clearly decided all this in his own mind, he was well on the way toward doing so when, in May of 1942, he sent Eisenhower to England with General Mark W. Clark to observe and report upon the growing American military establish-

American troops move inland near Algiers, opposite, in Operation Torch. Ike had hoped that Admiral Jean Darlan (above, center, with Ike and Mark Clark at Allied headquarters in North Africa) could persuade the French not to resist the Allied landing—but the troops were fired upon in spite of Darlan's orders.

ment there. Returning to Washington ten days later, Eisenhower reported serious deficiencies in command arrangements, recommended the immediate establishment of a European theater, and then prepared a proposed "Directive for the Commanding General" of the suggested theater. When he presented this directive to Marshall personally, the Chief of Staff, after glancing through it, asked its author if he was satisfied with it. Eisenhower said he was. "That's good," Marshall said, "because you're the man who is going to execute it. . . . When can you leave?"

Eisenhower arrived in London on June 23. He was assigned a suite in Claridge's, the swankiest of London hotels, but was uncomfortable amidst so much luxury ("I feel as though I were living in sin," he complained). He soon had an aide find more suitable quarters in the Dorchester on Park Lane, across from Hyde Park. Only three short blocks separated it from 20 Grosvenor Square (soon dubbed "Eisenhower Platz" by war correspondents), where the commanding general had his office.

One of the first things he did was work out with the American Office of War Information and the British Ministry of Information ways and means of establishing good relations between American troops and the British public. The American soldiers had snappier uniforms and higher pay than their British counterparts; they had more and better food than the severely rationed British civilians; and they were, in their ignorance of British character and of what the British had endured since 1939, inclined to patronize a people who (in turn) regarded them as latecomers into a war necessary for the common survival, a war in which the British had for a long time stood alone against the common enemy. There were abundant opportunities here for ugly incidents that might be fatal to the kind of Anglo-American cooperation necessary for victory. That Eisenhower should recognize this as a problem of prime importance, and address himself to its solution (it was solved) as his first major act in his new assignment, was indicative of his accurate sense of relative values.

In his relations with his own staff, and everywhere within range of his personal and official influence, he preached and practiced Allied unity as if it were, as indeed it practically became, an article of religious faith. He made himself a living symbol of such unity.

Marshall took happy note of this when on July 18 he arrived in London for the crucial strategy conference. He may have noted too—and perhaps with a certain chagrin amidst his general approval—how careful Eisenhower was during that conference to avoid any "taking of sides" that might alienate either the Americans or the British who were engaged in the talks.

For, as it turned out, Marshall had suffered an unmitigated personal defeat by the time this meeting of the Combined Chiefs of Staff had ended on July 25. The final decision was that North Africa would be invaded (in an operation code-named Torch) no later than October 30 (the date was later advanced to November 8) and that the invasion of France, though preparations for it should continue, would be staged in 1943 only if "a marked deterioration in German military strength" became apparent "and the resources of the United Nations, available after meeting other commitments,"

Eisenhower (right) confers with General George S. Patton in March, 1943.

Greeted by shouts of "Long live America," Patton's Seventh Army rolls into Palermo twelve days after the Sicily landing.

permitted it. In effect, then, the 1943 invasion of the Continent was canceled. And there was (for Marshall) unhappy irony in the fact that Torch—initially proposed by the British and opposed by the Americans—must nevertheless be primarily an American operation. It was therefore up to Marshall to name the American commander of this Allied expedition—and he had no hesitancy in naming Dwight Eisenhower.

There followed weeks of wrangling between the British and Americans over the strategic shape that Torch should have. The British wanted the whole of the Allied expeditionary force to be landed inside the Mediterranean—at Oran, Algiers, and Bône (the easternmost landing)—in order that Tunisia, the strategic objective, could be seized within a couple of weeks or, at most, four weeks. The Americans, fearful of a failure in this first trial of American arms, concerned lest Franco's Spain close the Strait of Gibraltar after the Allied forces were inside the sea, thus severing the Allied line of communications, wanted one major landing on the Atlantic coast in French Morocco so that no matter what Franco did, the forces landing on the northern coast would have at least one door opened at their rear through which supplies and reinforcements could come. This meant the elimination of the Bône landing. In the end, the matter had to be settled directly between Roosevelt and Churchill, who decided in favor of a Casablanca landing, in addition to those at Oran and Algiers, instead of the Bône landing near Tunis, which the British staff had favored.

Eisenhower's tactic throughout this controversy was to avoid taking any side at all. But if his compromising spirit contributed little or nothing toward the resolution of this strategic issue, it greatly helped him to develop the actual means—the Allied fighting force—by which strategy must be realized in battle. By the time the issue was finally settled in late August, he had gone far toward developing a command system and process unprecedented in the history of military alliances. He had fused Americans and British into a single efficient, smooth-running staff that was imbued with his own sunny good will and his own (and Marshall's) conception of Allied unity. The effective amalgamation of nationalisms he thus achieved was matched by a no less difficult amalgamation, at the top level, of different armed services—naval and ground forces, the air forces, the services of supply. He refused personally to decide staff issues until every possibility of staff agreement had been exhausted; he sometimes had staff sections virtually locked into an office together until they either arrived at a solution or proved absolutely that they could not. By word and example he promoted attitudes of selflessness and cooperation.

The remarkably happy and harmonious command arrangement that emerged from this was all the more remarkable for being achieved amidst the most acute frustrations and anxieties. There was not enough of anything—ships, men, matériel, or time—to permit the North African operation to be launched with any real margin of safety. There were many worrisome imponderables born of a complicated political situation. The Free French, who might have been counted upon to aid the enterprise, were being rigorously excluded from all knowledge of it, partly on grounds of security but mostly because of the American Government's diplomatic recognition of Vichy France as a sovereign power and the personal animosity that the Free French leader, General Charles de Gaulle, aroused in Roosevelt and the top officials of the State Department, especially Secretary Cordell Hull. Despite the State Department's recognition of Vichy, no one could say whether or not the Vichy French in North Africa would oppose the landings: if they resisted with all the strength at their disposal, even complete tactical surprise would not insure success. The risk was increased by continuing uncertainties about the reaction of Spain.

On November 5, Eisenhower and his immediate staff flew to Gibraltar, where his headquarters was established in the tunnels of the historic rock. Three task forces comprising a million tons of shipping—until then the greatest amphibious force ever committed to a single operation of war—had sailed several days before, en route to the landing beaches. On November 8 all three landings were successfully made. There was no real resistance at Algiers, and the resistance at Oran, while bitter, was quickly overcome. The stubbornest resistance was at Casablanca, though even there the issue was never in doubt. It was upon this Western Task Force that the greatest anxieties of the whole expedition had been focused. Normally at that time of year there is high surf upon the African Atlantic coast (this was one reason for British opposition to landing there). But the sea was relatively calm when the Allied forces went ashore, and after three days of heavy fighting, the Vichy commander of Casablanca, realizing his position was hopeless, surrendered. On that same day, November 11, German forces (unresisted by forces under Vichy orders) marched into and occupied theretofore Unoccupied France.

By then a race was under way between Anglo-American forces pushing toward Tunis and the buildup in Tunisia of German forces brought in by ship and plane from Europe. Simultaneous with it and intensified by it was a continuation of the political difficulties born primarily of the State Department's long wooing of Vichy and its repulsion of de Gaulle's Free French.

Eisenhower's chief adviser on North African political affairs at this time (as during the planning stages of Torch) was an American career diplomat named Robert D. Murphy, American Consul General in Algiers. Murphy was excluded by State Department policy from a consideration of de Gaulle or any other Free Frenchman as a leader to whom the North African French might rally. He had perforce looked elsewhere and had been persuaded, and had persuaded Eisenhower, that an elderly French general named Henri Giraud, a hero of World War I, could fill this role. Murphy was badly mistaken. Smuggled out of southern France and brought to Gibraltar by submarine, Giraud had made difficulties for Eisenhower on the eve of the invasion (he had come believing, perhaps on the basis of promises made to him, that he was to *command* the operation); the most forceful language had been required to persuade Giraud to enact, or attempt to enact, the role assigned to him. He had then broadcast by radio from Gibraltar an appeal to his compatriots in North Africa, calling upon them to follow his leadership into the Allied cause, and had

In Sicily in 1943, the Eighth Army shells enemy strongholds in the Allied advance on Messina.

gone to Algiers, where it at once became clear that he had in fact no following whatever.

But it happened that there was in Algiers at the time of the landing a high, and much hated, Vichy French official, Admiral Jean Francois Darlan, commander in chief of Vichy's armed forces, of which the most important component was the powerful French fleet, anchored then at Toulon. Darlan had come to Algiers, it was said, to visit his son, stricken with polio. Murphy was convinced, and in turn convinced the American military, that Darlan might do what Giraud had so signally failed to do. He might do more: the French fleet might sail at his orders to join the Allies.

Accordingly, Eisenhower entered into what at once became notorious throughout the free world as the "Darlan Deal," whereby, in return for Darlan's presumed authority over the North African French, exercised on behalf of the Allies, Vichy officials were retained in office, and Vichy laws, including anti-Semitic decrees and laws suppressing civil liberties, were kept in force. There were thus set in train grave political troubles as an accompaniment to military events, troubles that continued into and beyond the time (in 1943) when the Americans and British were compelled to recognize through official acts the actual authority and prestige among Frenchmen of Charles de Gaulle.

Eisenhower justified this "deal" wholly on grounds of "military expediency." He believed then, and continued to say later, that by making it he had protected vastly extended and vulnerable lines of communication as his troops rushed eastward. But Darlan's orders to French officials in Tunisia to aid the Allies and oppose the German buildup—an order he issued only when forced to do so—had no effect whatever. Nor did the French fleet sail to join the Allies; instead, it blew itself up in what de Gaulle called "the most pitiful and sterile suicide imaginable." And the Allies' race for Tunis was lost. By Christmas, when heavy rains transformed Algerian and Tunisian fields into seas of mud, Allied forces were bogged down not far inside the Tunisian border, condemned to weary weeks and months of stalemate.

The remainder of the story, though long in happening, may be swiftly told. Eisenhower's forces, having suffered, and then recovered, from a major tactical defeat at Kasserine Pass in February, began to make significant advances in March. In April, they were linked up in southern Tunisia with General Bernard Montgomery's Eighth Army, which had driven all the way from Egypt since its victory at El Alamein early in the preceding November. Montgomery and his army then came under Eisenhower's command. The final offensive followed in early May. Tunis was taken by the Allies on May 7, and six days later the German and Italian forces, who had retreated into the Cape Bon peninsula, surrendered unconditionally. It was a famous victory. The enemy lost 340,000 killed, wounded, or captured. A total of 1,696 enemy aircraft were destroyed, and 633 were captured intact on the ground, as compared with a loss of 657 Allied planes. Ninety-five enemy ships had been sunk by air attack, 47 by submarines, 42 by surface forces. In the meantime, on the other side of the Mediterranean, Italy was reeling from successive bitter defeats. Soon she would be knocked out of the war.

*President Roosevelt, returning from Cairo and Teheran in
1943, reviews Allied troops with Ike in Sicily. Shortly afterwards,
Eisenhower was named Commander of Allied forces in Europe.*

The Leader Emerges

by GENERAL MARK W. CLARK

General Mark W. Clark was Commander in Chief of U.S. Ground Forces in Europe in 1942. After the war he became chief of U.S. forces in Austria, and from 1952 to 1953 he commanded the United Nations forces in Korea. Here, he tells of his association with Eisenhower at the beginning of the war and the events leading up to Ike's appointment as Commander in Europe.

It was in the period just prior to and following the attack on Pearl Harbor that an old friend and fellow cadet at West Point became recognized as a potentially great military leader. I was in a position to watch this man come into focus as a commander of first rank, and it pleased me very much, for I had seen his qualities of leadership and of heart and soul required to lead men in battle while he was a cadet at the United States Military Academy. Ike was two years my senior at West Point, but we were in the same company and lived in the same division of barracks. We saw a lot of each other. In the late thirties he was the Chief of Staff for General Douglas MacArthur in the Philippines before returning in 1939 to Fort Lewis, Washington, to take command of a battalion of the 15th Infantry. At that time I was a major and G–3 of the Third Division stationed on the West Coast with its headquarters at Lewis. Here we had another opportunity to be together training troops for combat.

Again I saw his sterling qualities, but of course never foresaw that we would serve so intimately together as we were to do in World War II. No more did I foresee that he would be primarily responsible for the opportunities that were later to come to me.

As the war clouds gathered at the time of Pearl Harbor, our paths separated. I became the Chief of Staff to General Lesley McNair in Washington at G.H.Q., and Ike became the Chief of Staff to General Walter Krueger, commanding the Third Army at San Antonio, Texas. As my job in Washington was directly associated with building of divisions to meet the enemy, I was again in daily touch with Ike, doing the same job for the Third Army.

It soon became increasingly important to give these field commanders a chance to handle large units of troops in the field, and McNair wanted to test the soundness of our logistical doctrines in large-scale maneuvers, where men could sleep and live and work as near as possible under combat conditions. The Louisiana maneuvers were typical of such tests, and Walter Krueger's Third Army was pitted against General Ben Lear's Second Army. Here, Ike Eisenhower had his first opportunity to demonstrate his strategic concepts with a fine plan for making a huge envelopment around Lear's flank in order to get to his rear. It doubtless would have been a great success had we not limited the maneuvers to the state of Louisiana, which ruled out Ike's great plan for his envelopment through Texas.

As McNair's deputy for Louisiana field exercises, I conducted the critiques that followed these problems, and just as I was concluding one of them, an officer handed me a

telegram from Washington listing the names of a number of officers who had been nominated by the President for promotion to the grade of brigadier general. I took a quick look at it and noticed Eisenhower's name well up on the list. I took another quick look, and out in front I saw Ike sitting in the first row. It was too good a chance to miss. I announced to the officers in attendance that I had just received the list of promotions and would read the names. There was a silence as thick as a Turkish rug in the big recreation hall where we were meeting. I read the names, but when I came to Ike's I deliberately skipped it and read all the way through the list before I paused, studied the paper briefly, and added: ". . . and Colonel Dwight D. Eisenhower." He was watching me closely with bright, alert eyes, as if he might have been expecting something of the sort, and as I read his name he dropped one eyelid in a broad, pleased wink. I noticed as the meeting broke up that it was Ike who got the most congratulations.

It was not long afterward that General George Marshall, Army Chief of Staff, came down to observe our field training operations. One evening when we were sitting alone, he told me about certain changes he was making in the staff in Washington. "I wish you would give me a list of ten names of officers you know well and whom you would recommend to be chief of the Operations Division of the War Department General Staff," he said.

"I'll be glad to do that," I replied, "but there would be only one name on the list. If you have to have ten names, I'll just put nine ditto marks below it."

"Who is this officer of whom you think so highly?" he asked.

"Ike Eisenhower," I said.

"I've never met him," Marshall said, but he quickly added that he knew of Ike's brilliant record. Not long thereafter, Eisenhower was ordered to Washington as chief of the War Plans Division and was soon made a major general.

In the months that followed, the parallel nature of our duties kept us in close liaison.

A few months later, in early May of 1942, Ike gave me a ring and said he was flying to England the next day, on Marshall's instructions, to study the situation at first hand.

"Will you go along?" he asked. "We'll be gone about three weeks."

I quickly accepted the invitation and secured McNair's consent.

The next day we flew out of Bolling Field in Washington, and after experiencing delays caused by bad weather over the Atlantic, arrived in Prestwick, Scotland. But flight conditions were so bad that we had to take the night train down to London. We were quartered at Claridge's hotel, and we quickly got down to work, the main result of which was a recommendation by Eisenhower, in which I heartily agreed, that

a senior, and experienced, general officer, who was familiar with Washington's new plans for action in Europe, should be sent without delay to command large numbers of U.S. troops, who would soon be flooding the British Isles.

The next most important thing about the trip—or at least the thing that sticks in my mind most firmly—was our meeting with General Bernard L. Montgomery, who was then the general officer in command of the British Army in the southeast of England. This was known early in the war as the Invasion Coast because it was there that the German invasion had been expected for so many months. Monty was then engaged in maneuvers that had the code name of Tiger, a nickname that was often applied to the dapper and hard-driving little general himself in those days. An invitation was extended to Ike and me to observe the maneuvers, and we drove down to Monty's headquarters, where we were shown into a small office lined with war maps to await the arrival of the distinguished soldier.

He came in briskly, was introduced, and promptly began to orient us with a crisp lecture. There were several other officers in the room, and everybody gave his full attention to Montgomery's remarks. After a while, Ike decided he would like to smoke a cigarette. He quietly fished around in his pocket, pulled out a pack, and offered one to me. I declined with a shake of my head, but Ike lighted up. He had taken about two puffs when the lecture broke off in the middle of a sentence. Monty sniffed the air without looking around and in a loud voice asked: "Who's smoking?"

"I am," Ike said meekly.

"I don't," Montgomery said sternly, "permit smoking in my office."

Ike put out his cigarette, and the lecture proceeded. At the conclusion of that first meeting between Ike and Monty, we got a good laugh out of the incident, but not until we were well out of Montgomery's hearing.

A few weeks later we were back in Washington. General Marshall had a meeting with Eisenhower during which he confided to Ike that he was sending him back to England as the supreme American commander. Marshall later sent for me and asked for my recommendation as to who should be the U.S. commander in the British Isles. I promptly replied "Eisenhower." He then informed me that he had already told Ike he would have the command and had asked him whom he wanted as his principal subordinate in command of the II

Corps, soon to be sent to England. Ike said, "Clark." Marshall gazed at me speculatively. "It looks as if you boys got together. How soon can you go?"

On June 23, at 9:10 A.M., Ike and I again flew out of Bolling Field for our second trip to Europe. It would be several years before we would return, during which time Ike would have demonstrated to the world that he had the qualities to be the victorious Supreme Allied Commander.

Serving with Ike

by GENERAL OMAR N. BRADLEY

This recapitulation of a conversation with General Omar N. Bradley covers the years of his closest association with Eisenhower, from 1943 through 1945. Following his service in World War II, General Bradley served as Army Chief of Staff and Chairman of the Joint Chiefs of Staff.

Ike and I were in the same cadet company at West Point, so I saw him several times a day at formations. He was very well liked by everyone and was very active in class affairs. He was on the football team until he hurt his knee, and after that he was a cheerleader. He was also on the staff of the yearbook put out by the graduating class. We had a lot of good men in our class, but I don't think we looked ahead to wonder if Ike or any other one would attain high rank. You see, promotions came slowly at that time. In fact, some of the infantry officers were second lieutenants for as long as six years. If you were young for your class (as Ike was not, but I was), you thought you'd be lucky to become a colonel by the time you were sixty-four.

I didn't actually serve with Ike until 1943. I arrived in North Africa on February 24, just two or three days after the action at the Kasserine Pass started. I was at Eisenhower's headquarters in Algiers until the twenty-eighth, and then I went up to the front. You see, I was sent over there as sort of a personal observer, or representative, of General Eisenhower: he told me that he was not going to prescribe where I went, but he wanted me to take a look at things I felt he would want to see if he had the time. Following that directive,

I went up to the front to talk with some of the men who had been in the Kasserine fight. I wanted to find out how effective our equipment was and how effective our training was.

We were working on a shoestring in North Africa, defending part of a wide front thinly. In such a situation you're apt to get smashed somewhere, and that's what happened at the Kasserine Pass. But Ike wasn't discouraged. He came to the front frequently, at least once every week or ten days. He never gave direct orders to the men in the field, of course, but he liked to talk with them. I've seen him sit in the shade, leaning up against a tree, and sign autographs for three-quarters of an hour. I remember one time in France, while his

headquarters were still in London, he flew over to talk to me, and when we took him back to his plane, we got to talking to a bunch of enlisted men, and he started signing autographs. After half an hour, I finally stepped in and said, "Look, you'd better be getting back before dark." He certainly enjoyed talking to the men about where they were from and where they had gone to school and things like that whenever he had the chance.

I sometimes thought that if I had been in Ike's place, I

could not have put up with some of the things he had to put up with, and I've heard him say since that maybe he wouldn't have put up with some things if he had it to do over. But he got results. His ability to compromise enabled him to get the maximum out of the British—Montgomery, for example. He had to argue with Montgomery quite a bit. But when Ike finally got firm about something, Montgomery would always say "Yes" and go along with it.

Eisenhower went back to England some time in January, 1944. Before that, the plans for D-Day were more or less tentative. We had to wait for a decision from the commander —whoever he was to be. We assumed it would be an American, either General Marshall or General Eisenhower. The President finally decided that General Marshall could not be spared from Washington, so Eisenhower was designated.

All the intelligence pertaining to enemy units, the terrain, and so forth had been collected by the staff before Ike came. But after studying the information and the plans, he decided that it looked like too much of a shoestring operation, and he immediately started to broaden it. He increased the invasion force and asked General Marshall and the American Chiefs of Staff to strengthen the effort by bringing in part of the Navy from the Pacific.

I felt that it was imperative to drop airborne forces back of Utah Beach, but the plan was opposed by the British air officer in charge of the airborne operation; he felt that such a maneuver at that critical spot would be suicidal. General Eisenhower agreed with me that the whole invasion would be jeopardized if we eliminated the drop. As it turned out, the casualties at Utah, including the airborne people, were no higher, percentagewise, than those at Omaha Beach. We did have casualties, yes, but the mission was accomplished.

Of course the most difficult decision Ike had to make was to go when we did on D-Day. At the time I was skeptical, I must admit, because the weather was so bad. Yet it turned out to be a blessing because the German air forces could not pick us up coming across. The waves were so high, however, that I was afraid we would have trouble getting ashore. We did lose our floating tanks, on which we'd counted a great deal, because the waves were too high for them. But that was more than offset by the fact that we were able to attain considerable surprise. As a matter of fact, if we had waited two weeks, which was the alternative to going when we did, we would have run into a big storm that would have made a land-

ing impossible. We would have had to put it off for four weeks, and by that time our security might have been jeopardized because too many people knew about it.

Another crucial decision was whether or not we were going to let Montgomery make one single thrust north of the Ruhr toward Berlin. Ike was under terrific pressure from the British to let Monty go it alone, and he took a long time to make that decision. I think he felt Montgomery was wrong from the first, but he needed some backing on it, and he finally got it from the American Chiefs of Staff. So we advanced on a broad front. I personally think it would have been a great mistake to let Monty have his way. Suppose they had hit him in the flank with the twenty-six divisions they hit us with in the Ruhr? They'd have ruined him.

What made Eisenhower the right man for the job in Europe? Well, his ability to get along with the Allies and to make an allied force work was of great importance, and so was his broad knowledge of tactics and strategy. And of course there was his ability to make decisions. Even as a junior officer, he never hesitated to make decisions. When he was in charge of the Plans and Operations Division of the General Staff in Washington under General Marshall, he once ordered a whole division overseas without ever talking to Marshall about it. He felt that General Marshall had given him the job of putting troops in to fit requirements, so there was no need to check with the General before ordering the division abroad. That was in accordance with Ike's general theory: you give a man a job and leave him to do it. That's the way he operated with us; he told us what he wanted done instead of telling us how to do it.

Ike was very good at sizing up his subordinates, too. We always talked personnel when we got together. I would keep him informed of how various commanders were doing. There might be some outstanding colonel who I thought ought to be made a brigadier general later; if so, I would always clear it with him so that he'd know all about it before I sent the recommendation to him officially. And he would also call to my attention someone he thought was doing well.

He had two other qualifications you must consider, great mental and physical energy. He got around a great deal and was on the job all the time. I remember a conversation we had during the war. We said we were probably living three years of our lives in one year of combat. He was a soldier of many talents—and a man of many lives.

Churchill, who, with Roosevelt, was Eisenhower's joint superior, confers with his commander, above, in England.

Southwick House, below, served as
Allied headquarters for the planning of the
Normandy invasion. It was there,
while gale winds blew up on the Channel,
that Eisenhower made his decision
to push ahead with the largest amphibious
assault ever launched in a war.

III
OPERATION OVERLORD

It is of the nature of supreme strategic command that its major working attention should be focused not on the present battle but on the battle to be fought in the future. The North African campaign, the thrust up through Sicily and Italy into the Continent, the invasion of Europe from the west, all had been fought on the supreme-command level months before the shooting began, when basic decisions were reached concerning over-all strategy and the commitments to be made of men and matériel. The actual events, viewed from this level, appeared as a working out of predetermined patterns, divested alike of surprise and anxiety; control had passed into the hands of subordinate commands.

Of these three mighty invasions, the greatest of course was the cross-Channel attack of June, 1944, which was eventually given the most famous code name of the war, Overlord. But before it could be launched, or finally planned, or a commander picked to lead it, the other two had to be successfully waged. Moreover, a coordination of the three moves had to be achieved.

So it was that in mid-January, 1943, months before Tunis was taken, the Combined Chiefs of Staff met in Casablanca with Roosevelt and Churchill to determine what direction the war in the west should take. Immediately the old argument between Washington and London (which dated back to the spring of 1942) was resumed, in a somewhat different form. Since there was now no possibility of striking the Atlantic coast of France in 1943, the Americans wanted to husband their European resources for a launching of the great invasion at the earliest possible moment in 1944. They proposed to assume a generally defensive posture against Germany while taking major offensive action against Japan in the next twelve months. They continued to be suspicious of British motives, and such suspicions were not allayed by British insistence at Casablanca that a conquered North Africa must immediately be used as a springboard for the conquest of Sicily—and ultimately Italy. The British contended that this thrust into the "soft underbelly" was not a departure from the agreed-upon over-all strategy but, instead, an integral part of it. A logical prelude to Overlord, it would use up limited German resources and force a dispersal of German troops that could otherwise be concentrated to resist the invasion of northern France. The latter remained the climactic strategic stroke—the British said so as emphatically as the Americans.

The argument waxed hot, and often bitter, for several days. The upshot, predictable insofar as the African operation logically implied it, was the decision to invade Sicily with forces under Eisenhower's command as soon as possible following the Tunisian conquest. July, 1943, was set as the target date. It was also decided to establish at once a skeleton headquarters for the future supreme commander of Allied forces, whoever he might be. British General Sir Frederick E. Morgan was designated Chief of Staff, Supreme Allied Command (COSSAC) and assigned the top-secret task of preparing, with his staff, initial plans for the cross-Channel attack —an operation originally called Roundup. Finally, at Casablanca, on the closing day of the meeting, Roosevelt made his much-controverted statement that the war could end only with the "unconditional surrender" of Germany, Japan, and Italy.

Thus were determined the broad outlines of Eisenhower's immediate future, and soon after the conference ended, several of his staff officers were devoting their major attention to plans for the Sicily operation (code named Husky). Such plans became the major staff function during the final weeks of the Tunisian campaign.

On July 10, 1943, the greatest amphibious force in history up to that time landed spearhead elements of the British Eighth Army (to which were attached Canadian units), commanded by General Bernard Law Montgomery, and of the U.S. Seventh Army, commanded by General George S. Patton, at seven beaches in southeastern Sicily. Five weeks and three days later, the entire island was in Allied hands. It was true that the campaign had been "conducted against an opponent already committed to withdrawal," as Major H. A. DeWeerd wrote a few months later. It was also true that this withdrawal was, on the whole, successfully made: the Germans managed to conduct an orderly retreat and to escape with the bulk of their men and equipment to the Italian mainland across the narrow Strait of Messina. Nevertheless, the Allied victory was substantial. Valuable strategic ground was gained, 135,000 Axis troops (mostly Italian, ruthlessly used by the Germans to screen their own withdrawal) were captured, and 32,000 Axis troops were killed or wounded—all this at the price of 25,000 Allied casualties.

And the political effect was as the British had predicted it would be. Two weeks after the Sicily landings, Mussolini was deposed by the Fascist Grand Council and placed under arrest by a new government appointed by the king, a government headed by elderly Marshal Pietro Badoglio. Secret negotiations were begun at once between emissaries from Rome and from Eisenhower's headquarters. The negotiations were complicated by the fact that under Mussolini, Germans had infiltrated all but the very highest level of the Italian government, where in fact Il Duce himself had become virtually a captive of Hitler. Hence, the Italians, though anxious to surrender, wanted desperately to do so in circumstances that would save them from Nazi tyranny and prevent their land from becoming a battleground. They wanted guarantees that the Allies could come into Italy with sufficient speed and in sufficient strength to forestall a German takeover. No such guarantees could be given them; security would permit no detail whatever of forthcoming operations to be vouchsafed them. The terms remained "unconditional surrender"—and in the end the Italians were forced to accept them. It was then agreed that the surrender would be-

Trucks rumble into an ordnance depot, above, in England. With D-Day drawing near, the Allies built up the largest stockpile of military supplies in history for the assault. It totaled almost six million tons.

come effective on September 8, with simultaneous radio broadcasts of it by Eisenhower and Badoglio.

Meanwhile, plans were completed and final preparations made in Eisenhower's headquarters for the invasion of the mainland. On the night of September 3, against no resistance, Montgomery put two divisions of the British Eighth Army across the Strait of Messina into the Italian toe—the first Allied troops, other than raiders, to set foot on the Continent since the fall of Greece—and began to work his way up the boot. On the evening of September 8, Eisenhower made his broadcast of the Italian surrender, despite the fact that Badoglio had indicated he might not follow suit. He did, however, ninety minutes later, having no alternative, and then fled south into territory already occupied by the Allies, where he established the seat of his government. On September 9, the equivalent of four divisions of a newly formed U.S. Fifth Army (half of it British), under the command of General Mark W. Clark, began to go ashore at Salerno, just forty-five miles south of Naples. It was a risky operation. The enemy expected it and responded with massive counterattacks that dangerously constricted the beachhead, even threatened at one time to cut it in two, four days after the initial landings. But the threat was overcome; the beachhead was expanded. Reinforcements and supplies poured ashore as the drive to the north began. In early October both Foggia, with its great airfields, and Naples, with its great harbor, were in Allied hands.

But from the Allied point of view that was the last good battle news to come out of Italy for a long time. The Germans retreated to defensive positions in a country where the mountainous terrain greatly favored the defense, thereafter exacting a heavy price for every mile of ground relinquished to the attacking Allies.

By this time Eisenhower was by far the most famous of all Allied soldiers, an immensely popular figure on both sides of the Atlantic. He had earned the trust, the respect, the good will, of Churchill and Roosevelt as well as of the British and American military leaders who worked with him. He was popular with troops, to whose personal review he devoted much time and attention. He enjoyed, too, a favorable press. When General Patton had visited a base hospital in August of 1943 and abused two men suffering from battle neurosis (a synonym for cowardice as far as Patton was concerned), Eisenhower was able to persuade the newsmen to refrain from reporting the story. Patton had been one of the best ground gainers in Sicily, and Eisenhower—though he sent Patton a blistering reprimand—was concerned with saving him for future operations. (Inevitably, when the story became known some months later, it raised a greater storm of popular indignation than would have followed immediate full publication of the facts.)

Correspondents assigned to his headquarters were dealt with virtually as members of his staff. His "off-the-record" talks with them about present and future operations were conducted with a frankness and candor that surprised, delighted, and sometimes worried them. Prior to the Sicily invasion, for instance, he called in the correspondents and told them precisely what, where, and when the next operation was to be. He did so to prevent their writing "think pieces" that might give the show away, and in this he was successful, but the weight of such a secret was greater than most newsmen cared to bear. He formed warm personal friendships with some of the most famous journalists—John Gunther, Quentin Reynolds, Merrill Mueller, Demaree Bess—who were moved to present his portrait to the public in the most favorable light. All correspondents who knew him personally liked and admired him.

Among the general public, which awaited with impatience the opening of a second front in France, it had become quite common knowledge that the choice of a commander for the cross-Channel invasion lay between Eisenhower and Marshall. The decision between the two men was Roosevelt's to make. He found it difficult. His initial choice was Marshall, but when he announced this to his "inner circle," it aroused strong opposition from the other members of the Joint Chiefs, who feared the loss of Marshall's influence on global strategy. Roosevelt himself felt, as he later confessed to Marshall, that he "could not sleep at night with you out of the country." He then tried to have Marshall himself make the decision, but Marshall refused to commit himself.

There is reason to believe that Marshall's reticence was at least partially determined by an opposition of desire and judgment in his mind. What professional soldier would not have desired the glory, the assured place in history that would belong to the successful commander of the greatest military operation of all time? But judgment told him that in all probability he could best serve the Allied cause by remaining where he was. Marshall would certainly be more efficient as staff chief and member of the Combined Chiefs than Eisenhower could be during the planning and mounting of Overlord. He could bring to his dealings with the Executive and the Congress a detailed knowledge and a personal authority that Eisenhower would have to acquire in office. He could sustain Eisenhower in Europe more effectively than Eisenhower could sustain him.

Roosevelt may well have sensed that Marshall had arrived at this conclusion. At any rate he arrived at it himself after weeks of delay during which he was repeatedly pressed by Churchill (by Stalin too) to make up his mind. On December 5, 1943, in Cairo— as he, Marshall, and Harry Hopkins were on their way home from a meeting with Churchill and Stalin in Teheran—the President made his decision. He informed Eisenhower of it a few days later. The public announcement was made on Christmas Eve.

On January 13, 1944, Eisenhower arrived in London to take up his new duties. He found his headquarters staff concentrated in the heart of London, as they had been in the summer of 1942, his own office being the same as he had occupied then, at 20 Grosvenor Square. Soon, however, he had established the Supreme Headquarters, Allied Expeditionary Force (SHAEF) at Wide Wing, in a village just outside London, where rows of gray concrete one-story buildings huddled under green mounds of camouflage netting provided offices. Here the staff members, in Eisenhower's words, "quickly developed a family relationship."

He did not overstate the case. All who visited SHAEF from its earliest to its final days were impressed by the happy efficiency of this headquarters. The officers working there did indeed have

Hours before the D-Day landing, Ike and Montgomery review their men.

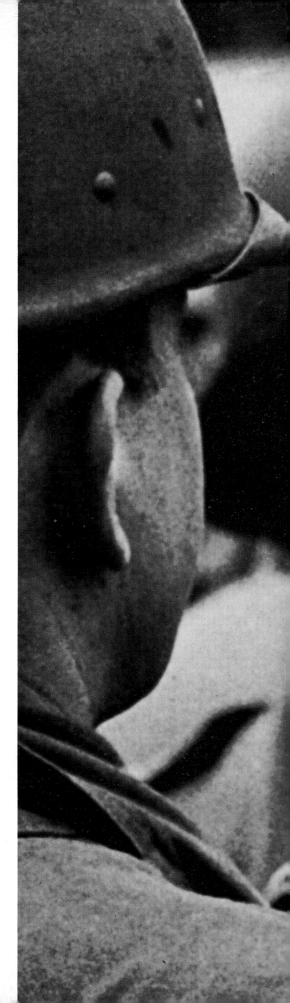

a fraternal relationship with one another: they took a family pride in the organization they served, and they were absolutely devoted to the Supreme Commander, whose demeanor of calm confidence set the tone of the whole establishment.

As for the organization itself, it was unique in military history. Eisenhower's Mediterranean headquarters provided precedents for much of it, but SHAEF was not only a much larger staff, it was also a more closely integrated one. Nationalistic differences were wholly submerged in it; and field commanders soon learned that it was profitless to argue against a SHAEF directive on the ground that it embodied an "American" or a "British" conception. Service differences were also submerged in SHAEF. Eisenhower's Chief of Staff was General Walter Bedell Smith, who had proved his worth in this capacity during the Mediterranean campaign. The Deputy Supreme Commander was British Air Chief Marshal Sir Trafford Leigh-Mallory. Naval Commander in Chief was British Admiral Sir Bertram Ramsay. No ground commander in chief was appointed, but General Montgomery in effect served in this capacity during the planning and initial operating phases of Overlord, working closely with American General Omar Bradley. Each of these commanders in chief played a dual role: he was both a staff member responsible for planning the operation and a top commander responsible for executing his assigned portion of the plan. The result was that ground, air, naval, and logistical forces were closely intermeshed. They worked together in reciprocal action, like gear wheels in a smooth-running machine that was lubricated by Eisenhower's personality and his insistence upon "cooperation."

The first sketchy outline plan for Overlord, seen by Eisenhower before he left the Mediterranean theater, called for a three-division amphibious assault upon the Normandy coast, with only two other divisions afloat at the time the assault was made. COSSAC had developed this plan on the assumptions that the attack must be launched on May 1, 1944 (once this date had been agreed to, the Americans were inclined to regard all British efforts at postponement as evidence of a lack of commitment to the operation) and that there would be a simultaneous landing of Mediterranean forces in the south of France—assumptions that, in view of the demands of the Pacific war, imposed stringent limitations on available shipping. Eisenhower was convinced the assault was being planned on too small a scale (so were Montgomery, Marshall, and Churchill), and in the end the decision was made to postpone the Normandy assault until early June and the southern France landing until a later date so that Overlord could be expanded from a three-division to a five-division attack. The selected landing grounds were five beaches scattered between the mouth of the Orne River and the eastern coast of the Cotentin Peninsula, at whose northern tip was Cherbourg, the first major Allied objective.

By late March, when troops and material began to move into staging areas, England was so weighted down with war goods that only the massed barrage of balloons held her above sea level, according to a wisecrack of that time. Nearly ten thousand war planes were parked wing tip to wing tip on dozens of airfields. There were scores of huge parks of carefully camouflaged tanks, trucks, bulldozers, "ducks," jeeps, self-propelled guns. There was more ammunition stacked along English roads than had been expended in the whole of World War I. Soon, dozens of ports were jammed with shipping: more than four thousand ships were to take men and equipment across the Channel, plus thousands of small craft, protected by a dozen battleships, scores of cruisers and destroyers, and hundreds of gunboats, corvettes, destroyer escorts, and other fire-support craft. Every day that weather permitted, beginning in early April as prescribed by the Overlord plan, Allied bombers swept over northern France, pounding the railroad system with devastating effect. Railroad marshaling yards were pulverized, between fifteen hundred and two thousand locomotives were destroyed, and of the two dozen bridges across the Seine between Paris and the sea, eighteen were broken and three others damaged. These raids were patterned in such a way as to indicate the Pas de Calais area, opposite Dover across the narrowest part of the Channel, as the invasion target area, a deception aided by the creation of a fictitious army group in East Anglia, where huge (though empty) cantonments and thousands of dummy trucks and vehicles, with dummy landing craft in the appropriate ports, were spread below the eyes of German reconnaissance planes.

By the first week of June, all was in readiness. Every risk that could be foreseen had been calculated and discounted. Every unit had been assigned its task, spelled out in detail, and had rehearsed its performance over and over again. The vast, intricate movement of the invasion forces and their supplies to the embarkation ports had been completed. There remained a single risk factor impossible to control or even to predict with desired certainty: the weather.

And on June 3, two days before the planned D-Day, this weather factor became worrisome indeed. There developed over the Atlantic what SHAEF weathermen described as a "typical December depression," which, moving eastward, meant high winds, high seas, and low clouds across the Channel on June 5. Landings would be difficult, naval fire support inaccurate, and air cover impossible. No airborne landings could be made. Early in the morning of June 4, after some of the ships were already at sea en route to rendezvous areas, Eisenhower met with his top staff members and the weathermen to review the situation. He decided that D-Day must be postponed for twenty-four hours, though this increased the chances of a security leak and might reduce the weight of the initial assault, since there was some doubt that troop-laden ships, called back to port, could be readied for sailing again in twenty-four hours.

On the evening of that same June 4, a day of rain and wailing wind, gloomy indeed for the Supreme Commander, the top staff members met again with the weathermen to review the decision to invade on June 6. Meteorologists now predicted an interruption of the "December" weather pattern. A high pressure area, moving northeastward from Spain, should clear the skies by the afternoon of June 5. The skies should remain clear or partly cloudy and the seas relatively calm on the morning of Tuesday, June 6, though in the afternoon clouds would probably form again. The storm might resume full force next day. Eisenhower asked his staff members for opinions. Smith and Montgomery favored keeping the June 6 date.

Coming ashore at Omaha Beach (above), American

GI receives a transfusion. German prisoners are

troops seek refuge from enemy fire behind anti-invasion obstacles. At left, below, the troops form to move inland. At right, below, a wounded

rounded up (bottom left) by two American soldiers while elsewhere (bottom right) British Seabees search for friends among heavy casualties.

Allied soldiers moved quickly across France after D-Day. A dead cow (top) provides a shield from fire; a tank (center) shells the Germans in the rubble of a French town. At bottom, a GI charges toward Cherbourg.

Opposite: General Charles de Gaulle leads marchers down the Champs Elysées celebrating the liberation of Paris.

Tedder and Leigh-Mallory were dubious. Ramsay stressed the fact that a postponement now would have to be for a minimum of forty-eight hours because of the need to refuel ships and that firm sailing orders must be issued at once if the June 6 date was kept; otherwise the ships that had farthest to go would not reach their destinations at the scheduled time. The final decision was now Eisenhower's alone to make. He decided that the invasion must proceed.

The fortunateness of this decision for the Allied cause was increasingly realized during the weeks that followed. The weather turned out to be as the meteorologists had predicted. The vast Allied armada sailed under broken clouds over moderate seas through the night of June 5 and the morning of June 6, and on D-Day all the landings were successfully made, the only grave difficulty being at Omaha Beach in the American sector. Here for a time the issue was in doubt; but here, as elsewhere, the beachhead was secured by nightfall, and troops were pushing inland. Then the weather turned bad, and it remained almost uninterruptedly bad (the worst weather to strike Normandy in seventy summers) through all of June. Had Eisenhower postponed the invasion, it could not have been made until July, by which time it would have been virtually impossible to achieve the complete tactical surprise that was in fact achieved on June 6. Moreover, the embarkation ports would have become the targets of a "secret weapon" with which Hitler began to attack England on June 13. This weapon was the V-I, a jet-propelled pilotless plane with a ton of TNT in its nose. When the motor cut out, the plane dove to earth, exploding on impact with terrific blast effect. It killed over five thousand people and caused heavy damage in London, especially during the first weeks of the attack, and might well have proved catastrophic for Overlord had it focused on the Portsmouth-Southampton area before the invasion got under way.

As it was, the continued heavy rains greatly hampered the offensive in Normandy. Supplies and reinforcements poured ashore; the attackers soon outnumbered the defenders by a wide margin. But the Allied advance through the Normandy hedgerow country, which was beautifully adapted to defensive purposes even when dry, fell far behind schedule as the weeks passed. After Cherbourg was taken in satisfactory time, on June 26, liberating the whole of the Cotentin Peninsula, the battle lines remained almost stationary for long periods. By mid-July there was widespread fear among the British and American publics that the Germans might manage to contain the bridgehead indefinitely, thereby nullifying its value.

This fear was fed by war correspondents whose dispatches also became increasingly critical of "command timidity" on the part of top Allied generals in France. In the initial stages of Overlord, Montgomery was in command of all the ground forces, but within a few weeks, as the rapid buildup proceeded, he and Omar Bradley were in effect operating on the same level under Eisenhower's over-all direction, Bradley being in command of the Americans on the right. Both commanders, if in different ways, were cautious men, concerned with keeping the casualties among their men at the minimum commensurate with the requirements of their as-

signment. Each was far less willing to assume major risks in order to achieve major victories swiftly than was, for prime example, General Patton. And Patton during this period was in full agreement with those who criticized the top command for a failure to move. He waited in the wings, so to speak, for his cue to move onto the stage of history, and he waited with growing impatience.

According to the command arrangement decided upon before the landings were made, all American forces in France were to remain in the U.S. First Army, under Bradley's command, until the Allies had broken out of their Normandy confinement. When that happened, the American forces were to be divided into two armies, the First and the Third, comprising the 12th Army Group, with Bradley as Group Commander. The First Army, under General Courtney Hodges, would operate on the American left where (as things turned out) it would face, in conjunction with Montgomery's 21st Army Group, the heaviest concentration of enemy armor and the strongest prepared enemy defenses. The Third Army, under Patton, would operate on the American right; armor-heavy and highly mobile, it was to execute a swinging right hook that would take the enemy flank and rear.

Not until July 15 did the Americans reach the line, from Saint-Lô west to the sea, from which the breakout assault could be launched—a line they had originally planned to reach by the fifth day after the landings. Not until July 25, because of days of stormy weather, was the assault actually made. But once made, it quickly scored the break-through, and on July 28 Patton actually assumed the Third Army command, which became officially his at noon on August 1. Thereafter, the Allied advance was swift indeed. While Hodges' army and Montgomery's forces pushed hard against major concentrations of German defensive power, Patton swept through Brittany, sent a flying column south to the Loire, sent other columns east to Le Mans, then north from Le Mans to Argentan, until the German Seventh Army, savagely pounded from the air, was almost surrounded. But not quite.

In the second week of August, Patton was halted by Bradley's orders at Argentan where, according to plan, he was to be met by British and Canadian forces coming south from Caen through Falaise, closing a steel ring around all the Germans in Normandy. The British and Canadians, however, came hard against prepared German defenses and were halted there while broken elements of the German Seventh streamed through a twelve-mile gap in the Allied line. By the time the trap was closed many thousands of enemy troops had escaped across the Seine.

The triumph was nevertheless a great one. In conjunction with the invasion of southern France by Mediterranean Allied forces on August 15, followed by swift advances up the Rhone valley against little resistance, the close of the Normandy campaign meant the liberation of all France. The Allies suffered some 170,000 casualties in the Normandy battle, between June 6 and August 19, but the Germans lost between 250,000 and 300,000 killed or captured, including twenty army, corps, and divisional commanders. The Germans also lost more than 1,000 tanks and 3,000 guns. Their retreat did not halt until they reached the German border.

Ike lines up with his Western Front generals in 1944. The first row includes Patton (at left), Bradley, Ike, Hodges, and Simpson.

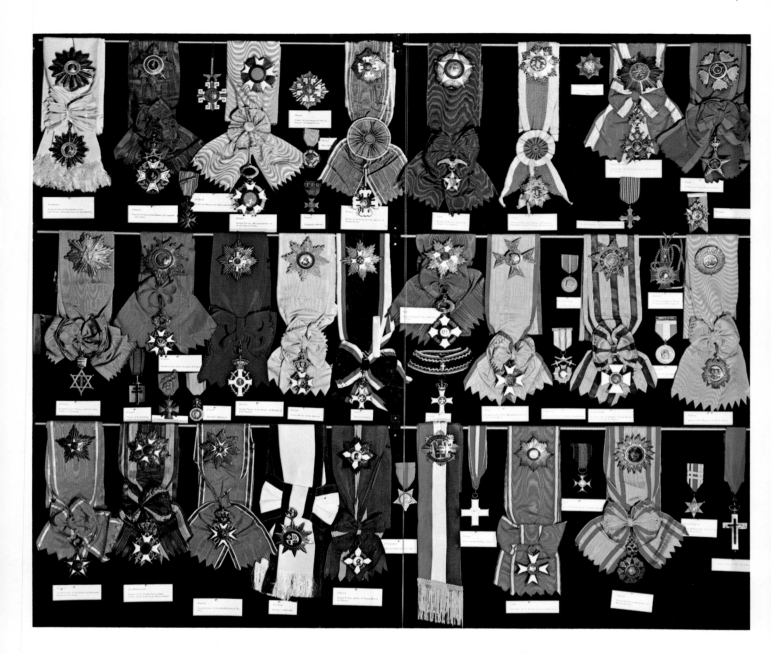

In recognition of Eisenhower's victorious leadership, many nations awarded him their highest honors. Above are some of the decorations he received. *Top row, left to right: Great Cross of the Order of the Liberator General José de San Martín, Argentina; Grand Cordon of the Order of Leopold with Palm, Croix de Guerre of 1940 with Palm, Belgium; Grand Cross of the National Order of the Southern Cross, Order of Aeronautical Merit-Degree of Grand Cross (top), War Medal (center), Campaign Medal (bottom), Order of Military Merit-Degree of Grand Cross, Brazil; Order of Merit-Degree of Grand Commander, Chile; Order of the Cloud and Banner, Grand Cordon Special Class, Republic of China; Order of the White Lion First Class, Golden Star of the Order of the*

White Lion for Victory (top), Military Cross 1939 (bottom), Czechoslovakia; L'Ordre d'Ismal, Grand Cordon (top), Egypt; Order of Abdon Calderon, First Class (bottom), Ecuador. In the center row, left to right: Order of King Solomon's Seal, Knight Grand Cross with Cordon, Ethiopia; Cross of Liberation, Grand Cross of the Legion of Honor, Croix de Guerre (bottom), Médaille Militaire, France; Grand Cross of the Order of George I with Swords, Order of the Redeemer, Greece; Cross of Merit of the Order of Malta; Military Order of Italy, Knight Grand Cross (top), Italy; Order of Malta (bottom); Grand Cross of the the National Order of Honor and Merit, Haiti; Médaille Militaire (top), Luxembourg; Cross of Military Merit First Class (bottom),

Guatemala; Grand Cross of the Order of the Oak Crown, Luxembourg; Order of Military Merit First Class (top), Medal of Civic Merit (bottom), Order of the Aztec Eagle First Class, Mexico. Bottom row, left to right: Grand Cross of the Order of Quissam Alaouite Cherifien, Morocco; Knight of the Grand Cross of the Order of the Netherlands Lion; Grand Cross of the Order of St. Olaf, Norway; Order of Pakistan; Grand Cross of the Order of Vasco Núñez de Balboa, Panama; Distinguished Service Star, Shield of Honor, Philippines; Order of the Grunwald Cross First Class, Chevalier of the Order of Poland Restored, Order of Military Virtue, Poland; Grand Cordon of the Order of Nichan Iftikhar, Tunisia; North African Star, Great Britain; Grand Cross of the Holy Sepulcher.

RECOLLECTIONS / III

Ike the Warrior

by BRIGADIER GENERAL S. L. A. MARSHALL

The following commentary on Eisenhower's generalship was submitted by Brigadier General S. L. A. Marshall, the eminent military critic and Chief Historian on the European Theater during 1944-45 when Eisenhower was Supreme Commander.

I am disturbed that with the passing years General Eisenhower's work and achievement as the director of Allied fighting forces in the European Theater has become no better understood by his own countrymen. In any company, to name him among the great battlefield captains is to invite skepticism. The fact is almost no one thinks of him that way. People take it for granted that his role was that of the Great Peacemaker, a veritable diplomat among generals, who needed only a ready smile and a firm handshake to resolve conflicting counsels and get governments to agree.

Yet from Operation Torch onward, his hand was directly in the design for battle—and he never knew defeat.

The plan that won Normandy was Eisenhower's own. He saw more surely than all others what had to be done, and because he stood his ground, the great invasion succeeded gloriously. Who now remembers that the lesser plan, which he was charged to execute, had already won approval from the Allied heads of government and the Combined Chiefs of Staff? By insisting that the invasion front be broadened and the force strengthened, he averted disaster. We who had the task of analyzing and recapitulating the strategies and tactics of World War II in Europe saw it plain as a pikestaff that his intervention in this matter was decisive.

It was his command practice to let his subordinates reap public credit that they might follow him more loyally. However generous, that tends to fuzz up history. Even the late General Walter Bedell Smith, his Chief of Staff and alter ego, did not dig to the root of that story in his book concerned with defining Eisenhower as a strategist (*Eisenhower's Six Great Decisions*). Alas, the historians have dug no deeper. So let us have at it.

In 1943 Eisenhower commanded in the Mediterranean. Normandy planning went on in the London headquarters of COSSAC (Chief of Staff, Supreme Allied Command) under the capable guidance of British Lieutenant General Sir Frederick E. Morgan. Sir Freddie was confident that an Allied expedition against France could defeat Hitler. But he had grave doubt of the commander designate—General Sir Alan Brooke. For many reasons, the planning already pointed toward Nor-

mandy. Sir Alan, though a doughty soldier, looked askance at that. When France was falling in 1940, he had brought the last British troops out through the Cotentin Peninsula's compartmented boscage, and the thought of going back to that maze chilled him. His gloom made Churchill no less wary.

When Secretary of War Henry L. Stimson visited England in the spring of 1943, Morgan confided his misgivings about Brooke. On returning to Washington, Stimson convinced President Roosevelt that an American must command the invasion. Stimson's own nominee was General George C. Marshall, but when that idea failed for various reasons, the final decision was deferred.

Eisenhower had heard nothing of this maneuvering when in September, 1943, he was visited by U.S. Major General William Chambers of the COSSAC staff who brought to Africa a copy of the invasion plan. Morgan wanted Eisenhower's reaction to it, since he was the only Allied general

with recent experience in large-scale amphibious operations.

Never guessing that his own fortune was at stake, Eisenhower went over the paper with Chambers, then said, "The attack on a three-division front is fatally weak. Were this my operation, I would insist on broadening it to a five-division front with two divisions in floating reserve."

Chambers returned that warning to Morgan. But COSSAC could not alter the plan as suggested because the troop basis and the available sea-lift did not permit any such expansion.

When in December Eisenhower was advised that he would be Supreme Commander, his overriding concern became the substitution of his own five-division concept for the smaller COSSAC assault. That he was under orders to return immediately to Washington for consultation served to double his anxiety about whether there would still be time to make the essential changes. If the force was to be approximately doubled, the beachhead would have to be broadened accordingly—which meant further surveys, more mapping, fresh loading plans, the pre-empting of additional shipping from the Pacific, and so forth.

So Eisenhower called General Sir Bernard Montgomery to his headquarters in Algiers and told him where he thought the plan was wrong. Since Monty readily agreed, he was asked to go to London at once and argue the case. "You will be right in telling them I will not yield in this matter," Eisenhower said. Then to strengthen Montgomery's hand, he sent General Smith with him as backer-up.

Monty's first port of call as messenger was Marrakech, since Churchill happened to be there on December 31, reviewing the plan for Operation Overlord, code name for the big show. The Prime Minister asked Monty for a critique of the plan, and next morning the General handed him a paper outlining the new concept, all essentials of which Eisenhower had put to Chambers four months earlier. Here is the basis for the claim that Montgomery masterminded the invasion by overhauling COSSAC's ideas of how to control the beachhead (an objective then called the lodgment).

The record says that the initial decision was made by the same man who later compelled higher authority to accept it. Monty and Smith still had not won their case by the time Eisenhower got to London. In fact, General Thomas T. Handy, speaking for the U.S. Joint Chiefs of Staff, trailed him to England, still trying to persuade him that the three-division assault front would be power enough. Eisenhower stood firm, and the opposition had either to yield or to relieve him. Of its yielding came the addition of the Utah Beach operation and the two-division U.S. airborne strike inland from it, which together proved decisive.

Let us note, however, that these were issues not in strategy but in grand tactics. The questions of where and when to strike had been settled, and no exception was taken to them. The dispute was over how to do it. Knowing exactly what he wanted to insure victory, Eisenhower energized revision of the plan. It was his design that converted the doubters and built the total confidence that was the touchstone of success.

"Beetle" Smith always felt that the greatest of Eisenhower's decisions was made at 0400 on June 5, 1944, when the Supreme Commander weighed the odds for five minutes and said, "Well, we'll go." Only three words, and the big show got under way. They were said after the chief meteorologist, Group Captain J. M. Stagg, forecast that the prohibitively rough weather, with its high winds and rough seas, would lift for only twenty-four hours. Hearing what he said, no subordinate had any advice to offer. Eisenhower had to think things through and decide all alone. He responded with the instinct of a gambler, lacking which, no battle commander may ever

get off the pivot. His decision was not only morally of the highest order; it required a lightning appraisal of what could be accomplished in such a brief interval. Eisenhower, the tactician, was at his best in that moment. For as it happened, decision in the landing did become nailed down within the first twenty-four hours.

The Normandy night-drop provides another startling example of his tactical judgment. The place where the bolder five-division plan was most likely to part at the seams was right next to Utah Beach. The U.S. airborne 82nd and 101st divisions were thrown into the venture to insure the winning of the beach before the seaborne 4th Division put out its small-boat waves just before dawn. That sturdy warrior, General Omar N. Bradley, who originated this part of the plan, said that to his tactician's eye the terrain allowed for no alternative.

Then, very belatedly, Air Chief Marshal Sir Trafford Leigh-Mallory tried to get the night-drop canceled, saying it would result in an 80 per cent loss of machines and men. Bradley, the realist, countered: "No airborne attack, then no Utah Beach assault."

Their head-on clash put Eisenhower once more on the hot seat. Alone in his tent, he weighed the decision, then confirmed the operation as set. It was a tactical ruling of the first order. Thousands of lives were at stake. More to the point, if Mallory was right, then the invasion was likely to fail everywhere. Eisenhower simply reckoned that Mallory had badly miscalculated. So he had. The drop losses were somewhat less than 4 per cent: over-all first-day casualties were about 10 per cent. The night-drop proved to be the linchpin of the whole operation, the decisive amendment to a COSSAC plan that without it would have been marked for defeat.

Clear vision combined with tough-mindedness are also reflected in Eisenhower's decision to stay with the air plan that called for the bombing of French railway centers throughout the two months preceding D-Day. The main object was to disarrange communications that might serve a German counterattack against the beachhead. The British War Cabinet urged Eisenhower to cancel the air raids, fearing that the killing of thousands of French civilians would alienate and outrage the population. So did General Koenig, who from England was commanding the French Forces of the Interior. So here was formidable political pressure combined with a soul-trying humanitarian appeal. Ike simply would not bow to it. What came of his stand in the end? French civilian casualties were remarkably light, and the confusion dealt the German enemy was tremendous. No bombing operation during World War II paid off more handsomely.

While the several episodes that I have cited are typical of Eisenhower's generalship, they only suggest its dimensions. One must read all of the conference papers and notes to understand the scope. Eisenhower and Smith worked together almost perfectly in tandem. Usually they saw eye to eye. Yet in argument they invariably supplemented each other, and the effect on the opposition was like a well-timed crossbuck in football.

There is a popular illusion that generalship can be measured by victory or defeat: were things that simple, Eisenhower would rate automatically as the great captain of the century. His every battle was a large affair; he knew nothing but success. No other command in history compares with his in numbers of people directed, magnitude of logistics, and duration of sustained effort. Behind it all was the "unceasing rumble of wheels, the whisperings of intriguing officials, the tumult of fears and hopes, of things growing, struggling, eluding the grasp, dissolving and then springing up again." At the center was his solitary figure.

Comrade in Arms

by VISCOUNT MONTGOMERY OF ALAMEIN

Viscount Montgomery of Alamein commanded the British Eighth Army in North Africa in 1942 and led Allied land forces in the invasion of Europe. He served with Eisenhower until the end of the war and again in 1951 as Eisenhower's Deputy Supreme Commander at SHAPE. Here, Montgomery recalls their friendship during their service together.

During the last week in May, 1942, I was directing large-scale maneuvers in southeast England for the divisions under my command; it was a very tough exercise, code name Tiger, and it is remembered to this day. Two American major generals were in England at the time, studying training methods, and they asked if they might visit me to see what was going on. The two were Dwight D. Eisenhower (Director of Military Operations) and Mark Clark (Director of Military Training) —both from Army Headquarters in Washington. These two were both to play a prominent part in Hitler's war from the end of 1942 onwards, and both became my firm friends.

On 7th August, 1942, I was ordered to take command of the First British Army, which was to land in North Africa the following November under Eisenhower's supreme command. But fate intervened. At 7 A.M. the next morning, the order was canceled, and I left England on the 10th August to command the Eighth Army—then facing Rommel's army at Alamein. I next met Eisenhower on the 31st March, 1943; the Eighth Army had fought its way from Alamein to Tunisia and was now under his command. I myself was to remain under his command until the end of the German war in May, 1945. Historians will in due course evaluate Eisenhower's ability in the realm of high command in war; I can, of course, make a contribution to that investigation. But first let me tell of our friendship—how it began and developed, how it almost died in October, 1958, and how all became well in April, 1965.

Eisenhower's strength lay in his human qualities. In some extraordinary way he could instantly warm the hearts of all who came into contact with him. He had a most disarming smile, and it was impossible to become exasperated with him however much one might disagree with his opinions or actions. A simple man, he was utterly sincere in all he did. During our long wartime association he was my chief and I was his subordinate. I never really knew what he thought of me in those days, but when he came to Paris in 1951 to take command of the NATO forces, and during his eight years as President of the United States, we became close friends. I often stayed with him in the White House and in his home at Gettysburg. He was a very great gentleman, with all that that implies.

In September, 1958, I was to withdraw from employment in NATO, and in May of that year I paid a farewell visit to America. The Pilgrims of the United States gave a dinner for me in New York on the 25th May, and Eisenhower sent a telegram to be read out at the dinner: "Please give my greetings to the Pilgrims of the United States and their guests assembled in honor of Field Marshal Montgomery. . . . Across the face of the earth he has served faithfully and tirelessly in the cause of mankind. I am delighted to have another opportunity to salute my old friend and comrade in arms." I was given the telegram to keep. Few soldiers can ever have received such a tribute; it brought tears to my eyes.

During the years following the end of Hitler's war, many books were published in which writers, civilian and military, gave their views in no uncertain voice about what went on during that war. Eisenhower was the first of the service chiefs to publish his account, in 1948; General Bradley followed in 1951. Although I came in for considerable criticism in both books, certain ungenerous statements being made, I remained

silent. In October, 1958, having by then withdrawn from active employment in NATO and in the British Army, I thought it suitable to give *my* account of the military operations in which I had played some part, and I did so in my memoirs— where I published, with Eisenhower's written agreement, the correspondence which had passed between us during the campaign from Normandy to Berlin. His feelings were hurt; he ceased all communication with me; I was greatly distressed.

Then in April, 1965, the B.B.C. produced a television program, "Victory in Europe—Twenty Years After," in which the chief actors were to be Eisenhower and myself—he in New York and I in London—talking via the Early Bird satellite. I decided to use the occasion to try and re-establish our former friendship, and I wrote to him—saying we were both getting old, we could not go on any longer in this way, let us speak to each other over the air and become friends again. His reaction was immediate and typical of the man: he agreed at once. I am so very glad it happened before it was too late.

Let me now turn to his military ability. By the very nature of things, skill in the profession of arms has to be learnt mostly in theory by studying the *science* of war—since practical experience in the *art* does not come often to the general. The great captains have always been serious students of military history. Whether Eisenhower had studied the science of war deeply, I do not know. But both are essential in order to exercise high command successfully—study of the *science* by reading, and practice of the *art* in battle. He most certainly lacked knowledge in putting the science to practical experience in battle: he had never seen a shot fired in anger until he landed in North Africa on 8th November, 1942, as a supreme commander, and he had never commanded troops in battle before that date. This I suppose is where we differed. I had been a serious student of the science of war and had also commanded in battle every unit and formation from a platoon to great armies. A clash of opinion was almost inevitable!

My first anxieties that some difficult times lay ahead were aroused during the operations in Sicily and Italy between July and December, 1943. Eisenhower seemed to me to lack the power of decision; he was dominated too much by his staff. The Allied campaign in Italy got into a mess—no grand design, no master plan, no grip on the operations, and a first class administrative muddle.

At the end of 1943, Eisenhower was transferred to London as Supreme Commander for the invasion of Normandy in June, 1944, and for the subsequent operations which were to bring about the defeat of Germany. I was delighted to be appointed to command the land armies under him. But my anxieties were increased when he himself went off to the United States, having first ordered me to go to London on the 1st January, 1944, and work out a plan for the Normandy invasion with the naval and air commanders in chief and have it ready for him later in the month. I was, of course, delighted, but it was not my way of exercising command. I reckoned he should have made the plan himself, or at any rate have directed the planning in its initial stages.

The story of the operations in Normandy is well known. I doubt if Eisenhower really understood the master plan for the Normandy battles. He was upset when his staff and the American press complained that British progress on the eastern flank of the bridgehead in the Caen area was too slow: why did not the British break out quickly towards Paris? He wasn't upset by the unfair criticism. Indeed, he agreed with it, and in July he went so far as to complain to Winston Churchill that the British and Canadians were not doing their fair share of the fighting on the eastern flank. He never could grasp the fact that *the master plan was for the Americans to break out on the western flank.* The British task was to draw the maximum German strength on to their front so that the American break-out would be possible—and this the British army group most certainly did. The slowness was an American fault; it took them a long time to get poised for the break-out battle.

The proper strategy for the Western Allies after the great victory in Normandy will be argued by historians for many years; they will find it a happy hunting ground. My views have often been expressed; they have never changed. I argued that by early August, 1944, we had drawn into battle, and defeated, south of the Seine, every German division in the west; the German air force had been shot out of the sky. We must finish off the German war by Christmas in order to ease the burden of the British people and to avoid further loss of life. To do this, we must concentrate sufficient strength to get decisive results quickly and then deliver a drive in great strength to secure bridgeheads over the Rhine and seize the Ruhr. This would entail halting a proportion of our force and diverting the necessary logistic support to the offensive punch.

Eisenhower did not agree. He said the whole allied line must advance on a broad front, from Switzerland to the North Sea, until the situation became clear. I pointed out that our logistic resources could not nourish such a movement. We would nowhere be strong enough to get decisive results quickly; the Germans would be given time to recover, and our advance would peter out; the war would go on into 1945, with all that would entail politically vis-à-vis the Russians advancing from the east; the additional loss of life would be severe.

Then, after the victory in Normandy, Eisenhower descended from the lofty perch of a supreme commander and assumed the additional burden of direct command of the land armies, a post for which he was not qualified. From that day the operations of the Western Allies began to go off the rails. We became involved in a long winter campaign during which manpower problems became serious in both British and American armies because of casualties. The German war did not end until May, 1945. The Russians got to Berlin, Prague, and Vienna before the Western Allies, with all that that was to entail for the future peace of the world—and we could have grabbed all three of those great political centers.

And so, while I had a tremendous affection and admiration for Eisenhower, and will always acclaim him as a very great human being, I find it impossible to include him among the great captains of history. But this can be said, and in no uncertain voice—nobody else could have carried the burden of Supreme Commander in the West in the way he did and kept the nations and the warring tribes of generals and air marshals working together to the end. For this alone the free world will always owe him a deep debt of gratitude.

Mopping up after Hitler's Third Reich,
American infantrymen and tanks advance toward
Wetzhausen, Germany, in April of 1945.

IV

VICTORY AND TRIAL

As Eisenhower's armies pursued the fleeing and disorganized German troops across the Seine and into Belgium the problem of supply over rapidly lengthening lines of communication became acute. Antwerp, taken so swiftly (September 4) that the Germans had no time to demolish harbor installations, could not be used as an Allied supply port until the Schelde Estuary, still in enemy hands, had been cleared. Spearheads driving north and east must continue to be supplied primarily from stockpiles built up in Normandy during the weeks of beachhead confinement and from the only two operating ports, Cherbourg and an artificial harbor near Arromanches, all hundreds of miles to the rear.

In these circumstances, Eisenhower was required to make a basic strategy decision of utmost gravity. Moreover, he must make it quickly if opportunity was not to be lost, for though the enemy's forces in the west were scattered, demoralized, and numerically weak in early September, they would not long remain so. The Germans had repeatedly demonstrated their ability to make rapid recovery from battle defeat; they still had disposable reserves within their country; and they were known to be frantically recruiting and training new divisions. If they could stop and hold the Allies along a prepared defensive line—and the Siegfried Line was certainly well prepared—they might prolong the war for many months and greatly increase the price of Allied victory.

Succinctly put, the choice facing Eisenhower was between a broad-front and a narrow-front strategy. Either he distributed Allied offensive strength fairly evenly between the southern and northern wings and continued to press forward in both areas or he concentrated in one area and went on the defensive elsewhere. If he made the latter choice, he must decide whether to concentrate his strength in the north, where Montgomery's 21st Army Group operated, or in the south, where Bradley's 12th Army Group was.

Montgomery, promoted to the rank of Field Marshal at about this time (only a few months before Eisenhower was promoted to the five-star rank of General of the Army) proposed a northern concentration. He was convinced that "a really full-blooded thrust" in that area might swiftly capture the Ruhr, the industrial heart of Germany's war-making power, and drive on to Berlin, ending the war before Christmas. He urged Eisenhower to assign him the divisions and the supplies he needed. This of course meant halting the advance on Bradley's front because there were simply "not enough maintenance resources for two full-blooded thrusts," as Montgomery kept insisting.

It might be expected that Bradley (with Patton) would regard this proposal with something less than enthusiasm, and in fact he bitterly opposed it. He argued that a "single axis of advance" would permit the enemy to concentrate defenses against it, whereas with a "double thrust" Eisenhower could "feint and dodge" and "confuse" the enemy, who would then be forced to stretch his defenses to the breaking point. The argument was not wholly devoid of malice. Bradley disliked Montgomery as a man (the British commander seemed to him insufferably egotistical); he had little respect for Montgomery as a general (the British commander impressed him as cautious to the point of timidity); and in private talk he made no secret of his opinion that Montgomery, granted the resources he requested, would not strike swiftly enough, boldly enough, to achieve decisive results. Hence, Bradley's initial opposition to the single-axis idea was so vehement that he could not accept it even when Montgomery, though convinced that the richest strategic ground was in the north, suggested as an alternative that the thrust be made in Bradley's own sector while the 21st Army Group did "the best it could with what was left over."

Never more clearly than at this juncture, in all his military career, did Eisenhower demonstrate his conciliatory nature and his consequent reluctance to make an unequivocal choice between mutually exclusive alternatives. On the record, he was at first inclined to support Montgomery's conception. To British vehicles and tanks he diverted gasoline that would otherwise have fueled Patton's Third Army armor (how Patton fumed!)—and it must be said that Montgomery then belied his alleged incapacity to move swiftly. British spearhead units covered nearly two hundred miles in four days to seize Antwerp. Eisenhower then gave Montgomery permission to bypass German forces controlling the Schelde Estuary so that the British drive could continue north and east. Over Bradley's protest he approved Montgomery's conception of an airborne operation whereby a bridgehead across the Lower Rhine might be achieved at Arnhem, outflanking the Siegfried Line. But he refused to commit himself to the one full-blooded-thrust concept insofar as it required him to halt all southern offensives; he refused to reduce Bradley's command to a single army so that Montgomery would have the forty divisions which, in the British view, a left-hook knockout required. Nor would he accept the alternative proposal that he launch a hard straight right through the Saar Basin and beyond, in Bradley's sector.

The argument continued even after the airborne operation (Market-Garden) was under way. To settle it, Eisenhower called a strategy conference at his Versailles headquarters. There, on September 22, he decided to back Montgomery's original plan. He ordered Hodges' U.S. First Army to support Montgomery's right wing, thus giving Montgomery most of the divisional strength he had been asking for; he ordered "the remainder of the 12th Army Group to take no more aggressive action than is permitted by the

Grim Allied commanders, with Ike at center, inspect a German concentration camp. Had there been any question before whether the Allies were engaged in a "crusade," the uncertainty vanished upon exposure to such scenes of horror.

maintenance situation after the full requirements of the main effort have been met." But by this time German Field Marshal Walter Model "had miraculously grafted a new backbone on the German army," as Bradley later put it, and had, moreover, augmented forces with which to resist the Allied offensive. The airborne operation gained ground valuable for the defense of Antwerp but failed by a narrow margin to achieve its ultimate objective. Of the 8,000 airborne troops dropped at Arnhem, 2,400 survivors were evacuated with great difficulty after British tank spearheads were halted south of the Waal River. The Siegfried Line was not outflanked; the Allies were condemned to months of bloody attrition warfare.

It was interrupted, this relatively static warfare, in mid-December—but by the Germans, and in a way initially frightening to the Allies. To concentrate strength for offensives in the north and south, Eisenhower had to permit the eighty-mile defensive line across the Ardennes to be stretched thin indeed. A mere four American divisions held it—two of them weakened by recent heavy battle, two of them without any battle experience whatever. Opposite them, the enemy, moving at night and aided by cloudy weather that prevented air reconnaissance, secretly massed in wooded country three armor-heavy armies comprising no fewer than twenty divisions, with another five divisions in close reserve. Early in the morning of December 16, the enemy attacked, achieving complete tactical surprise. The American front line was overwhelmed; within three days the attack had split the 12th Army Group in two, making it impossible for Bradley, from his headquarters south of the bulge (the battle became known as the Battle of the Bulge), to exercise effective command over the U.S. First and Ninth armies north of the bulge. Eisenhower therefore transferred these armies from Bradley's to Montgomery's command, and it was primarily with troops under Montgomery's orders that the German penetration was finally halted east of the Meuse and then, beginning on January 3, rolled back by an Allied counteroffensive.

The bulge battle was Hitler's last desperate bid for victory in the west. He had hoped to keep the Allies there on the defensive until the new jet fighting planes, then just coming into production in German factories, were available in sufficient numbers to sweep Allied bombers and fighters from the skies, and until long-range rockets had been perfected for attacks on Allied bases. He succeeded only in delaying for six weeks the launching of the planned air offensive; the cost was 82,000 irreplaceable troops and hundreds of irreplaceable tanks, planes, and guns. Moreover, by the time Eisenhower's ground offensive got under way (February, 1945), the Germans had been forced to make massive withdrawals from their troop strength in the west in order to meet the threat from the east, where a stupendous Russian offensive, launched on January 12, drove forward relentlessly. By that time, too, the Allied air offensive—especially the specific-target bombing of railroad communications, aircraft plants, ball-bearing plants, and the like—had inflicted mortal wounds on the German war economy.

What remained of German strength west of the Rhine was defeated by early March when (March 7), in one of the great fortunate accidents of the war, a bridge across the Rhine was captured intact,

With jubilant shouts, Allied prisoners dash toward freedom. They were among 6,000 liberated at Bad Orb by the advancing Seventh Army.

Montgomery (at left), Eisenhower, and Marshal Zhukov toast the Allied victory at a gathering in Berlin, above, in 1945. Opposite, jammed around a statue of George Washington in New York's Wall Street, Americans celebrate V-E Day.

breaking the last strong defensive line in the west. Allied forces poured across into country beautifully suited to swift offensive movements. Thereafter, a single anxiety remained amidst the joy of victory at SHAEF. This was that Hitler might establish (as his propaganda asserted he already had) an Alpine National Redoubt in Bavaria into which he and his fanatical followers would retreat and maintain themselves perhaps for years, punishing attackers with dreadful "secret weapons." The myth (for so it proved to be) was responsible in some measure for Eisenhower's highly controversial decision in late March to halt his eastward drive at the Elbe, after American armies had cut through the heart of Germany, so that major forces could be diverted to the conquest of Redoubt Alps. Thus the Americans would be waiting on the Elbe for a linkup with the Russians while the latter, driving westward, captured Berlin. Churchill protested bitterly after Eisenhower had communicated his decision in a personal message to Stalin, but by then it was a *fait accompli*, and one that, after all, was consistent with Roosevelt's effort to reduce Russia's distrust of the West.

Roosevelt regarded Big Three accord as absolutely essential to the creation of a permanently peaceful postwar world; he believed that his personal working relationship with Stalin, carefully fostered at Teheran and Yalta and through frequent direct messages, would enable such accord to be achieved. And who can say that what he wished for might not have happened if he had survived the war? He died on April 12, 1945, just as the last German resistance was collapsing. His successor, Harry S. Truman, was a very different kind of man—more combative, impulsive, impatient, addicted to blunt speech where Roosevelt had used soft words, inclined toward snap decisions where Roosevelt had postponed decisions until "things" had been given every chance "to work themselves out." Moreover (incredibly), Truman had not been briefed concerning Roosevelt's hopes and plans for the postwar world or on other matters of crucial importance, including the atomic bomb project.

The war's end came swiftly. On May 7, at 2:41 in the morning, in Eisenhower's headquarters in Reims, France, the instrument was signed which surrendered unconditionally all German forces, wherever they might be. Near midnight on May 8, this instrument was ratified with Russian signatures in Berlin.

Eisenhower of course knew, long before the war ended, that he had become a world figure. Once in Normandy, in August of 1944, a correspondent asked him about his postwar plans. He had none, he said; he couldn't think that far ahead. What he would like to do was travel around the world, visiting far places he had not yet seen—"Only," he added ruefully, "I can't see what good that would do anyone." His indication that "anyone" might thus affect his future, requiring him to "do good," was a tacit acknowledgment that his fame might to some degree become his master.

But if he had an inkling, he had no true idea of the dimensions of his fame until he finally encountered it in the weeks following V-E Day. In London, on June 12, he was given the greatest welcome ever accorded by that ancient capital to one not of English birth. White horses drew his open carriage through streets lined

by cheering millions to the Guildhall where, having been granted the freedom of the city, he made a speech that was printed and greatly praised throughout the world. "Humility must always be the portion of any man who receives acclaim earned in the blood of his followers and the sacrifices of his friends," he said. In Paris, on Bastille Day, more than a million Parisians cheered him as he was paraded in an open car to the Arc de Triomphe. There he was presented with a medal by General de Gaulle, and he responded to a toast of friendship from de Gaulle with an earnest one of his own: "There have been differences—you and I have had some. But let us bring our troubles to each other frankly and face them together.... Let's be friends." He was flown to Washington. Thirty thousand voices roared "Ike! Ike! Ike" as he stepped from his plane in the late morning of June 18 at the National Airport, and hundreds of thousands of people cheered his slow progress in an open car up Pennsylvania Avenue to the Capitol where he addressed a joint session of Congress. "...the banners of victory cannot hide from our sight the sacrifices in which victory has been bought," he said. "...[the soldier] knows that in war the threat of separate annihilation tends to hold allies together; he hopes we can find peace a nobler incentive to produce the same unity...." The next day he was flown to New York. Four million people cheered him as he rode through thirty-seven miles of streets to City Hall, where a gold medal was presented to him by Mayor Fiorello La Guardia. He was also made an honorary citizen of the city. He said: "It is not enough that we devise every kind of international machinery to keep the peace. We must also be strong ourselves. Weakness cannot cooperate with anything. Only strength can cooperate." Three days later, shortly before noon on June 21, his plane landed at Kansas City, Missouri. Again hundreds of thousands cheered him as he was driven in parade three miles through the heart of town to the Liberty Memorial of World War I. Here he addressed an immense throng: "This [the Middle West] has been called the heart of isolationism," he said. "I do not believe it. No intelligent person can be an isolationist...."

That evening he rode a special train along tracks that had carried him eastward when, thirty-four years ago almost to the day, he left home to enter West Point. Crowds gathered at every station along the way from Kansas City to Abilene where, when he descended, the crowd pressed so hard against him that he turned pale. He slept that night in his boyhood home; his brothers were there, and his aged mother. And next day he was the focus of the greatest celebration in the town's history. Abilene, whose normal population was five thousand, contained that day twenty thousand people, most of whom heard the speech he made in City Park, now named Eisenhower Park, following a parade in which floats depicted the history of the town and of the Eisenhower family. "No longer are we here independent of the rest of the world. . . ." he said. "Our part is most important. There is nothing so important to the world today as food in a material way. Food is necessary all over Europe and must be sent to preserve the peace. In that way you see immediately your connection with the problems of Europe. . . ."

There emerges from all this a fairly clear conception of how

Crowds line the sidewalks to welcome Eisenhower on his return to Kansas City in June of 1945.

*Changing military for civilian dress, Ike,
the new President of Columbia University,
dons a school tie before a football game.*

Eisenhower, obviously after much pondering, had decided to use the immense fame that had befallen him. He would use it to promote domestic unity and international cooperation for peace. As at SHAEF, his well-beloved personality (a British observer once remarked that Ike's lopsided grin was of itself alone worth many divisions to the Allied cause) and his naturally kindly and conciliatory disposition would become the medium of friendly understanding, the cement of mutual agreement, among otherwise diverse points of view and conflicting interests. In his public self, he would remain a unifying symbol, a ceremonial figure above the immediate battle, standing for all that was best in the American dream.

Hence the vehemence with which, at his Abilene homecoming, he responded to a question concerning his possible entry into politics. "In the strongest language you can command you can state that I have no political ambitions at all," he said. "Make it even stronger than that if you can. I would like to go further even than Sherman [who said that if nominated he would not run, if elected he would not serve] in expressing myself on this subject."

But of course his disavowal of personal political ambition did not prevent others from being ambitious for him, or for themselves by means of him. He had the magic power of being certainly elected President if only he would run or permit himself to be run; it was a magic that strongly appealed to leading members of both parties, since the General had no acknowledged party preference and indeed (it was said) had never voted in a national election. He returned to Europe, where he commanded United States Occupation Forces in Germany until November, 1945. He then became U.S. Army Chief of Staff, a two-year tour of duty that, he admitted privately at the time and publicly later, "was frankly distasteful." He had to preside over "a precipitate, almost helter-skelter" Army demobilization, a "unilateral disarmament" he deemed "unwise" even in those years before the deepening hostilities of the Cold War. He had to fight for the Army's plan against the Navy's plan for unification of the armed forces, a controversy from which the Navy emerged victorious. He also met defeat on his proposal for universal military training. And all through this period, politics and politicians pursued him relentlessly. As the election year of 1948 began, Southern Democrats wanted him as their presidential candidate. So did the liberal Americans for Democratic Action. So did leading elements of the Republican party, though definitely not that party's right wing, whose candidate was Senator Robert A. Taft.

He was forced by these pressures to search his own soul. He became less certain what he should do, less certain of what he wanted to do, than he had been at the time of his Abilene homecoming—and even then, however much he might have liked to go "further than Sherman" in rejecting political office, he had not actually gone as far. To friends he expressed doubt that he had a "right" to go that far. As a patriotic American, was he not obliged to serve his country in whatever capacity he was called upon to serve? He inclined to think so. Was there not a "mess" in Washington, as was so often asserted? His experience as Chief of Staff left him open to the conviction that there was. And was there not a danger that the country, facing difficult world challenges, might

Eisenhower was appointed President of Columbia University in June, 1948. At left, in cap and gown, he attends commencement exercises at the university. Below, Ike, an ex-halfback, reviews the Columbia squad.

again try to retreat into isolationism? He believed so. If he could "clean up the mess" and insure a rational internationalism simply by permitting his countrymen to make him President, was it not his duty to grant that permission? There were many who said it was—men of substance whose judgment he was bound to respect.

Some of the anguish of this soul searching was revealed to discerning eyes by a public statement he issued on January 23, 1948, in response to a letter from a New Hampshire newspaper publisher who wished to enter him in that state's Republican primary. He mentioned the difficulty of phrasing a statement that refused the political offer without at the same time "appearing to violate that concept of duty to country which calls upon every good citizen to place no limitations upon his readiness to serve in any designated capacity." He then expressed his conviction that "the necessary and wise subordination of the military to civil power will be best sustained, and our people will have greater confidence that it is so sustained, when lifelong professional soldiers, in the absence of some obvious and overriding reasons, abstain from seeking high political office." Politics, he went on, "is a profession; a serious, complicated, and, in its true sense, a noble one. In the American scene I see no dearth of men fitted by training, talent, and integrity for national leadership. On the other hand, nothing in the international or domestic situation especially qualifies for the most important office in the world a man whose adult years have been spent in the country's military forces. At least this is true in my case."

Eisenhower's decision insured the nomination of Governor Thomas E. Dewey of New York by the Republican convention in June, but between that time and the opening of the Democratic convention in mid-July, there was a sudden increase of pressure upon the General to run as a Democrat. He was forced at last to issue another statement: "I . . . could not accept nomination for any public office or participate in a partisan political contest." This seemed to insure Dewey's election, for Truman ran as the candidate of a party whose Southern right wing had been split off by the civil rights issue and whose left wing was presumably being split off by the third-party (Progressive) candidacy of former Vice President Henry A. Wallace. Truman's victory in November came, therefore, as a stunning blow to the Republicans and caused increasing numbers of them to turn again, almost desperately, to Eisenhower as their great hope for 1952.

And Eisenhower was now in a position much more vulnerable to such appeals. Even as he made his January, 1948, statement he was preparing to leave the office of staff chief (Bradley succeeded him), retire from the Army, and accept civilian employment as president of Columbia University, a position in which the late Nicholas Murray Butler had been perennially available (if he had not actually run) for the Republican presidential nomination. In the meantime, early in the spring of 1948, Eisenhower wrote his memoirs, *Crusade In Europe*. The book's publication that fall, some months after he had assumed his new duties at Columbia, heightened his prestige with the literate public (nearly all the reviews were solid raves) and earned him a great deal of money.

There were soon indications that Eisenhower was not wholly at

Appointed NATO chief in late 1950, Ike leaves for Europe with Mamie.

ease in his new role of university educator. He seems never to have been wholeheartedly accepted by a majority of Columbia's faculty or student body; he was much criticized for aloofness from them, for inaccessibility; and his public speeches, which seemed to many to sound increasingly like those of a Republican candidate for President, did not endear him to the intellectual community. He spoke out most strongly against big government and the "trend in thinking among our people, particularly the young" toward the conclusion that the Federal Government should solve every individual's every problem and "that hard work on the part of the individual was no longer the key to his own social and financial betterment." Then, in late 1950, President Truman asked him to return to active military duty in order to assume command of SHAPE (Supreme Headquarters, Allied Powers, Europe), whose task was to create effective military forces for NATO, headquartering in Paris. Eisenhower accepted.

In Paris, in this new assignment, for which his SHAEF experience had well prepared him, he did a first-rate job. The Allied military force was quickly and efficiently organized, and he became a spokesman (under the tutelage of Jean Monnet) for a United States of Europe. Simultaneously, his rejection of politics became much less emphatic, if indeed it was a rejection at all. To other arguments that he should run as a Republican was now added the apparent fact that he, and only he, could "save the two-party system," now threatened with extinction after twenty years of Democratic administration. By the end of 1951, few could doubt his availability for the presidential nomination. There remained some doubt as to whether he was a Republican or a Democrat until, on January 6, 1952, Senator Henry Cabot Lodge, recently returned to the United States from France, where he had visited Eisenhower, held a momentous press conference. Lodge said that the General was a Republican, that the General would accept the Republican nomination if offered, and that this statement would not be denied.

Next day, Eisenhower, besieged by reporters, made his reply. He did not say flatly that he was a Republican; he said that Lodge's announcement "gives an accurate account of the general tenor of my Republican voting record." He did not definitely approve political organization in his behalf; he said that "Of course there is no question of the right of American citizens to organize in pursuit of their common convictions." He did not clearly say that he would accept the nomination; he said that Lodge and the others had a right "to attempt to place before me next July a duty that would transcend my present responsibility," which, he stressed, was of great importance to the free world. His one unequivocal statement asserted that "Under no circumstances will I ask for relief from this assignment in order to seek nomination for political office, and I shall not participate in the preconvention activities of others who may have such an intention with respect to me."

Nevertheless, on April 11, 1952, the White House announced approval of Eisenhower's request to be relieved of his NATO assignment on June 1 and to be transferred to the retired list without pay. In early June he began a campaign to obtain votes at the Republican convention; his chief competitor was Senator Taft.

*Eisenhower bids farewell to General Alphonse
Juin, and to NATO, in May, 1952, in ceremonies at
NATO's Fontainebleau headquarters.*

RECOLLECTIONS / IV

Allied Commander

by EARL ATTLEE

Earl Attlee, former Labor party leader, was Prime Minister of Great Britain from 1945 to 1951, and until 1955 led the Opposition party. During the war he served as Deputy Prime Minister. Shortly before his death in 1967, Earl Attlee wrote the following comment about General Eisenhower.

There are few more difficult tasks than that of being commander in chief in war of a mixed force made up of contingents drawn from different races or different nationalities. Even more difficult is that of commanding troops belonging to different sovereign states, allies in war for the time being. Historically, perhaps the outstanding example of success is that of the great Duke of Marlborough, but there are several examples in the Second World War. Field Marshal Slim, for example, in the Burma campaign commanded British, Indian, and East and West African units and also managed to keep on good terms with the redoubtable "Vinegar Joe" Stilwell. General Alexander in Italy had to command contingents from more than twenty different nations. But the extreme example is that of General Eisenhower, and the remarkable qualities he displayed as commander in chief first in North Africa, later in the campaign against Italy, and finally in the Normandy landings—and the defeat of Hitler on the Western Front— put all the freedom-loving nations in his debt.

Not only had he to coordinate the forces of Britain and the United States but he had to see to it that the land, sea, and air forces worked in close harmony. History shows how often great enterprises, like the Walcheren expedition, failed through quarrels between the admirals and the generals. General Eisenhower, when given this assignment, had the disadvantage that he had had little experience of commanding large units in the field and lacked the prestige which comes from a great reputation. He had subordinates like Generals Montgomery and Patton, who were themselves strong personalities, while in the higher field of strategy he had to deal with great men such as Churchill and Roosevelt. On the other hand he was fortunate in having to deal with a body, the Joint Chiefs of Staff, which, thanks to men like General Marshall and Sir John Dill, had already achieved great cooperation.

First let us consider the nature of the assignment with which he was entrusted, the invasion across the narrow seas which separate Britain and Europe onto a hostile shore. Never since the close of the Middle Ages had this been attempted. Philip of Spain failed. Napoleon after weeks of waiting gave it up. Hitler after Dunkirk postponed and finally abandoned Operation Sea Lion. It involved weeks of careful planning in which land, air, and naval forces were involved. It meant that staffs both American and British had to work out together most meticulous details in planning. The seizure of a major port was out of the question. A novel enterprise had to be planned, that of throwing troops ashore on open beaches, troops some of whom had to be brought from other theaters of war and others from across the Atlantic. It required the closest cooperation between naval, army, and air staffs and their commanders and also eventually with the men of the Resistance movement in France. Clearly, in order to get the right spirit into all those engaged, a great deal depended on the Commander in Chief, General Eisenhower. He had to make the major decisions. He was completely successful. He

too had to make the bravest and most vital decision of all as to whether or not to give the order to start despite the doubtful weather prospects. This needed the highest moral courage, and fortunately, Eisenhower possessed just this.

In the later stages of the war Eisenhower was criticized for failing to advance more vigorously, thus allowing the Russians to penetrate so far to the west, with the result that Rumania, Bulgaria, Czechoslovakia, Hungary, and Poland all fell under Communist control, and it required great efforts to save Turkey, Greece, and Austria from suffering the same fate. But this may well have been due to the policy of President Roosevelt, who to the end of his life was obsessed with the view that Britain was still an imperialist power and that every move eastward was dictated by the old selfish interests.

I was always rather sorry that Eisenhower, who had become such a father figure in America, allowed himself to be exploited by the Republican party and to stand for President. No doubt it was a natural temptation to be like Washington, first in peace and first in war, but there were other examples, notably that of Grant, to warn him of the danger of a soldier meddling in politics. As it was, he was something of a *roi fainéant* as President, with Dulles as mayor of the palace.

In all my meetings during the war, and afterwards when I visited him at Gettysburg, I always found him the same simple, straightforward man; the world will not forget his great services to humanity.

Drafting Ike

by WILLIAM E. ROBINSON

William E. Robinson, former publisher of the New York Herald Tribune, *and former President and Chairman of the Coca Cola Company, was one of the organizers of Citizens for Eisenhower. Here he describes the events leading to Eisenhower's nomination for the Presidency in 1952.*

During the early part of General Eisenhower's work at NATO, his political party preference was unknown except to a few intimate friends. Consequently, during this tour of duty, he was under constant pressure by both major political parties to declare himself and return to the United States to run for the Presidency. Truman (as revealed in Eisenhower's book *Mandate for Change*) had offered to support him as the Democratic candidate for any office, including the Presidency.

In October, 1951, the leading Republican newspaper, the New York *Herald Tribune*, came out for his nomination on the Republican ticket. Thomas E. Dewey, during his campaign for governor of New York in 1950, called for Eisenhower as the presidential candidate for 1952. Senator Henry Cabot Lodge flew to NATO in September, 1951, to convince the General that he should be the Republican candidate—as the only one who could win. Ike pointed out to Lodge, as he had to others, that he "was not interested." The Senator persisted, asking permission merely to enter the General's name in the upcoming primaries. To this proposal, the best response that Lodge could get out of him was "I'll think about it." A small group of Republican members of the House sent him a message promising their support.

But the Democrats, in power and numbers, put on the greatest pressure. With no outstanding candidate in the offing, they were glad to go outside their professional ranks for a new leader. This was not the case with most Republicans. It was interesting to find out at this time that private polls taken among the Senate and House members in Washington showed an overwhelming preference for Taft among the Republicans, with Eisenhower as the majority choice among the Democrats.

To all the pressures from both political camps the General gave not the slightest encouragement. Rather it was distracting and sometimes annoying as he worked day and night and traveled extensively in Europe to build NATO into the effective Soviet deterrent it was to become.

During those days, I traveled to Europe frequently in connection with the business of the European edition of the *Herald Tribune* and other matters. I talked with Eisenhower on each of these visits, occasionally as his house guest.

From our conversations I clearly discerned two prime motivations for his refusal to support efforts in his behalf by either political party. The first of these was his strong conviction that NATO was absolutely essential as a defense against a Communist take over in Western Europe and his feeling that this service transcended any other that he could render his country and the freedom of the Western world. His second motivation was more personal, and one must understand General Eisenhower's almost unbelievable modesty and lack of egotistical instinct to realize this. Only those few who knew his innermost nature would ever understand why the lure of honor and glory in the Presidency meant little or nothing to him. His greatest hope after his NATO tour and later retirement as President of Columbia University was to live out his life with Mamie, his family, and his close friends. It was not that he was already satiated with honors, glory, applause, and parades. These things had never really touched him as they did other men. He did not want more of what meant little to him, and he would never, therefore, miss any of the kudos for which most men strive.

On one of my visits with him at NATO, he once remarked, "I've seen enough of political life in America as well as the world to know that it's very difficult to hold high political office without sacrificing principle. The greatest privilege and luxury I've had in my life is to be able to live and work by my principles. Other men may like money, glory, honor, but this is my particular treasure." I could only reply, "Wouldn't it be a great example for the future if someone *should* conduct political office on high principle? Maybe you're the one to do it."

During the Christmas holidays of 1951, when I was General and Mrs. Eisenhower's house guest at Marne La Coquette, the General agreed to let me say that he had voted Republican in the 1950 New York State elections. (We needed this for the first Republican primary in New Hampshire, since the voters there are required to swear to their party affiliation before voting for their choice of candidate.) That evening, over a drink before dinner, the General gave me an angry look, saying, "Why do I have to do this thing?" Although he was still determined not to campaign for the nomination, he knew the significance of the statement about his 1950 vote. The next day, as I gleefully prepared to fly back to the United States with the message, I went to Mrs. Eisenhower to say good-by, and this usually sweet-natured and gracious lady looked at me and said, "Bill, what are you trying to do to us? I don't think I should ever speak to you again." She fully shared General Ike's reluctance to enter political life—was probably the only American woman who had no desire to be the First Lady. Yet we never had a more gracious, modest, or beloved one.

Senator Lodge, who had been operating as an unofficial manager of the limited campaign for Eisenhower's nomina-

tion, had been told earlier by General Lucius Clay that General Ike was a Republican, but Lodge wanted Ike's permission to say so. On my return, I passed the word to Lodge. Two days later he had a press conference in Washington and officially labeled Eisenhower as a Republican. The campaign in New Hampshire for the write-in vote got into full swing. Meanwhile, Sherman Adams, New Hampshire's governor, had been working without portfolio and almost single-handedly to develop Ike's candidacy for the forthcoming March primary. In the opinion of the pros, Taft had the New Hampshire primary "locked up" and they considered Adams' effort to be silly and futile. However, Adams, by jeep, bus, and often on snowshoes,

worked throughout the state during one of the most bitter winters the region had ever known. On primary day he carried the state for General Ike by 46,661 to Taft's 35,838.

Now the pressures on Ike to resign his NATO post and return to campaign for the nomination became more intense. One of the General's oldest friends, who had become strongly involved in the movement to nominate him, made a special trip shortly after the Lodge announcement, to *demand* heatedly that Ike return. He said it was now a matter of duty to the nation and he had no right to shirk it. One of the few outstanding Republican leaders who had endorsed the Eisenhower candidacy sent a message that if he did not return to campaign for the nomination by March 1, the whole thing was hopeless. To these and other strong entreaties and ultimatums, Ike politely and simply said he still did not seek the office, had asked no one to work in his behalf, and could understand if they gave up the effort. There was no question but that General Ike would have been more relieved than disappointed if his proponents had given up.

But there were a few others (most of them amateurs) who felt that he should *not* return to campaign for the nomination. They knew that Ike was sincere in his conviction that he assume political office only if the people wanted him. To campaign for the nomination, making the usual political commitments and promises to the party professionals with the usual pleas for personal favor, was inimical to General Ike. Also, if he resigned his NATO post before he completed the organization job, the Democrats would accuse him of failure on the job and selfish political ambition. Ike's amateur friends were confident that the people's pressure on the Republican bosses and the delegates would be the only certain (if unprecedented) way to the nomination.

What was not generally known at this time was the long-term effort by a few of us to build the Eisenhower strength in key areas throughout the country. Indeed, among those who knew nothing of this was General Ike himself. For example, I started my own crusade in 1945, quietly building Ike cells in major cities throughout the country. I first spoke with business acquaintances in various cities and urged them to build a nucleus of Eisenhower supporters. These often included leading Republican contributors who had become a bit disillusioned after twenty years about the futility of sending good money after bad. They desperately wanted a winner, and they believed, with me, that we needed a popular nonpolitician.

The nature of my affiliation with the *Herald Tribune* had enabled me to know leading publishers, editors, writers, and artists. Directly or through mutual friends, we promoted the Eisenhower cause to the Scripps-Howard, Hearst, Knight, and other newspapers as well as to the leading magazines. Columnists such as Lippmann, Alsop, Lawrence, Drummond, and Krock were eventually to become strong factors in the development of public opinion for General Ike.

In addition to support from leading chains, the drive for the nomination was assisted by such influential newspapers as the New York *Times*, the Kansas City *Star*, and the Los Angeles *Times*. The Eisenhower war record, his understanding of foreign affairs and personalities, his universally appealing nature and behavior, his obvious integrity—all these elements helped break down the blind anti-Republican philosophy of the liberal writers and editors, many of whom had tagged Taft as an isolationist and Truman as a ward politician—whether unfairly or not.

When the Citizens for Eisenhower organization became a public fact in the summer of 1951, there was, therefore, an underlying nucleus of previous building behind it. When two young amateurs in New Jersey, Charles Willis and Stanley Rumbaugh, began to organize Ike clubs, they were remarkably successful from the beginning. The Citizens for Eisenhower had become by June 1, 1952, the strongest and best-financed amateur political force the nation had ever seen. Because of the outstanding character of its local leaders, it had great influence on the delegates as well as the professional political elements behind them.

Those responsible for the financing of this group included the late W. Alton Jones, Clifford Roberts, Sidney Weinberg, John Hay Whitney, and Ellis D. Slater. The administration of the national Citizens for Eisenhower was in the hands of General Lucius Clay, Paul Hoffman, Walter Williams, Mary Lord, Sigurd Larmon, and Bradshaw Mintener.

Strong as this movement was and as influential as were the leading publishers, editors, and writers, the nomination could not have been possible without the selfless work of such political experts as Governor Dewey of New York, Herbert Brownell, Senator James Duff of Pennsylvania, Sherman Adams, Senator Lodge of Massachusetts, Governor Arthur Langley of Washington, Senator Frank Carlson of Kansas, and Governor Dan Thornton of Colorado.

General Eisenhower had in late 1951 fixed the date of his return to Columbia University as June 1, 1952, feeling that his task at NATO would be completed as of that date. On June 4 he resumed his civilian life with a home-coming celebration at Abilene, Kansas. By this time he was, like it or not, a full-fledged candidate for the Republican nomination. The strong Taft trend had been slowed down by the primary write-in votes in New Hampshire and Minnesota. The professional group teamed up with the Citizens for Eisenhower to produce a hard-hitting political organization that gained daily in delegate strength against the front-running Senator Taft.

The home-coming Abilene television speech was delivered in the rain before a group of hardy townspeople standing in the fast-deepening mud in the local ball park. By five o'clock—speech time—the mud was ankle-deep in most places on the field. Altogether, this was an inauspicious beginning. Only a fire and brimstone speech could have overcome the miserable conditions, and Ike's speech was generally a disappointment.

Since TV had thus had its day, the newspapers eagerly awaited their opportunity on the following morning when the General was to hold a press conference in a local theatre without benefit of radio or television.

I had flown to Abilene with Joseph McConnell, then President of National Broadcasting Company and now President of the Reynolds Metals Company. To the consternation of my newspaper colleagues, Joe worked with his people at N.B.C. and his competitor at C.B.S. by telephone to get the networks cleared for Ike's press conference. And I, a newspaperman, worked with Ike and his staff in a traitorous endeavor to permit a telecast of the newspaper press conference. At midnight, General Ike agreed; Joe had the time cleared, and on this occasion, the General was in top form. The question and answer session was a great success and helped to wipe out the negative impression of the previous day.

During the ensuing month, until he arrived for the convention at Chicago on July 5, the General made several speeches. A number of delegates visited him at Denver and New York. In the speeches and in conversations with delegates, he simply stated his political philosophy and outlined the principles on which the nation should solve its problems and take advantage of its opportunities. He attacked no one; he curried favor with no one; he made no promises to special groups; he asked no one to vote for him at the convention.

As one delegation prepared to leave after a long session of questions and answers, the chairman said, "General, don't you have anything else to say to us? Don't you want to ask for our support?" Ike replied, "No, I have only one word of advice and that is, 'Let your conscience be your guide.'"

The story of his nomination at Chicago is well known, and I shall not repeat the details here. The public had achieved the political miracle of nominating a presidential candidate. General Eisenhower was probably the only candidate of either party since George Washington who was nominated without obligation or political commitment to anyone. President Eisenhower's appointment of cabinet officers, Supreme Court justices, and bureau personnel was unprecedented in that it had no taint of cronyism or political favoritism.

And that same unusual high principle and integrity characterized General Eisenhower's behavior in the election and throughout his administration.

Thousands of enthusiastic Eisenhower supporters gather in Texas, below, with songs and banners proclaiming "We Like Ike."

V

WE LIKE IKE

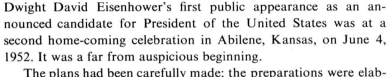

Dwight David Eisenhower's first public appearance as an announced candidate for President of the United States was at a second home-coming celebration in Abilene, Kansas, on June 4, 1952. It was a far from auspicious beginning.

The plans had been carefully made; the preparations were elaborate. In the morning, his boyhood home, purchased by leading citizens, was to be dedicated as a historical monument; the cornerstone of the Eisenhower Museum building, which was to rise on what had once been the family garden plot, was to be laid. In the afternoon, Ike and Mamie were to review a parade of high school bands, other marching groups, and a series of floats depicting his life. The climax was to be a nationwide radio and television address broadcast before a huge throng gathered out-of-doors at five o'clock. The managers of the affair, remembering the first home-coming seven years before, confidently predicted an attending crowd of twenty to forty thousand.

A small fraction of that number actually appeared. Storm clouds were gathered above Abilene as Eisenhower, at the cornerstone laying, asked his listeners this question: "If each of us in his own mind would dwell more upon those simple virtues—integrity, courage, self-confidence, an unshakable belief in his Bible—would not some of these problems tend to simplify themselves? Would not we, after having done our very best with them, be content to leave the rest with the Almighty and not to charge all our fellow men with the fault of bringing us where we were and are? I think it is possible that a contemplation, a study, a belief in those simple virtues would help us mightily." At noon, rain began to fall, one of the heaviest downpours of the year, and all afternoon rain fell, dampening bodies and spirits alike. The park was a sea of mud, and a light rain was still falling when Eisenhower, facing an array of empty seats and a few hundred bedraggled listeners, began his televised address. What he said, and the way he said it, did nothing to cheer his supporters. He looked old and tired before the camera eyes as, haltingly, without evident conviction, he spoke words prepared for him by his speech writers. To quote his own later summary, he said that "maximum productivity ... demanded a favorable industrial climate provided by government" as well as "intelligent cooperation among capital, management, and labor. . . . I put myself on record as an enemy of inflation and expressed the conviction that excessive taxation could destroy the incentive to excel."

He came out against "the evil of centralization of government and against dishonesty or corruption in any of its levels" and for an America that was "spiritually, economically, and militarily strong."

Addressed to a divided and trouble-ridden America (there was, above all, a longing to end the seemingly hopeless and certainly bloody Korean War), such words only gave comfort to his sole serious rival for the nomination, Senator Robert A. Taft. Nor did Eisenhower's public performance next morning improve his prospects, in the anxious view of many of his friends. At his first frankly political press conference, held in an Abilene theatre, he answered specific questions with generalities through which reporters searched in vain for a good news lead, although some of the men committed to him were convinced that the essential moral goodness of the man showed through his sometimes rambling words.

As for Eisenhower himself, there is evidence that he suffered a shock of disillusionment at Abilene and in the days immediately following. Five months before, he had said emphatically that "under no circumstances" would he "participate in the preconvention activities" of those who sought to nominate him. He had said it as one who, solely from a sense of duty and against his private desire, would heed a call to political service provided that call was clear and unmistakable. But at this time he had been told over and over again that he had only to announce his availability to be assured of the nomination. Now it appeared that this was not so. A majority of the hard-core Republicans, those animated by rigid conservative principles, were Taft men, and they had control of the convention machinery. They had named the keynote speaker (General Douglas MacArthur), the temporary chairman, and the permanent chairman. More importantly, the conservatives dominated the Republican National Committee, which was responsible for making up the temporary roll of delegates to open the convention—and according to convention rules adopted in 1948, each delegate on the temporary roll, even if his seat were contested, could vote on the seating of all contested delegates except himself. There were three states—Texas, Georgia, and Louisiana—where Taft and Eisenhower delegates both claimed seats. This meant that unless the rules were changed, Taft would go into the convention with well over a hundred more votes than Eisenhower had; on the first ballot he would be only 70 or 80 votes short of the 604 needed for nomination. Obviously, Eisenhower would have to fight for the nomination.

To millions of thoughtful Americans at that time, the contest appeared to be one of principle. Eisenhower was the progressive who cared primarily for human rights and stood for an enlightened internationalism; Taft was the archconservative who cared primarily for property rights and stood for a neoisolationist nationalism. Indeed, it seemed to many that Taft's formerly hard personal integrity had become distorted by his long-denied and now desperate ambition, so that it contrasted sharply with Eisenhower's. One of the most admirable things about Taft in the past had been his firm commitment to fair play in politics and to freedom of speech and thought as the very essence of true individualism. But in that year, he appeared to have formed a loose working alliance with Republican Senator Joseph R. McCarthy, then nearing the high

Eisenhower faced two opponents in 1952: his rival for the nomination, Senator Robert A. Taft of Ohio (above), known as "Mr. Republican"; and his Democratic foe, Adlai E. Stevenson (below). He beat them both, taking the nomination from Taft on the first ballot and the election from Stevenson by 442 electoral votes to 89.

Opposite, Ike opens his campaign on a drizzly day in Abilene.

tide of an incredible career. Like McCarthy, Taft charged that Communist agents were active in the Democratic Administration, and he rather more than implied that the Korean War (he called it "Truman's War") was the result of internal subversion. He blamed the victory of Chinese Communists over Chinese Nationalists upon "Communist infiltration" of the Far Eastern division of the State Department. This lent credence to vicious attacks made by McCarthy and Republican Senator William E. Jenner of Indiana upon General George C. Marshall as a Communist dupe if not an actual traitor (Jenner in a Senate speech called Marshall a "living lie"), since Marshall had been sent by Truman on a special mission to strife-torn China at the end of 1945 and had subsequently become Truman's Secretary of State. A Taft who achieved the White House on those terms could hardly be counted upon to curb McCarthyism's dangerous excesses. Eisenhower, on the other hand, whose immense personal prestige obviated the necessity to gain votes by appeals to irrational fears and suspicions, could be expected to sustain an official rejection of McCarthyism with a personal dislike of McCarthy and Jenner as men.

Thus the issue between the two candidates for the Republican nomination as seen by millions of Americans—and hence the excitement with which they watched the contest through the rest of June and early July. Eisenhower participated intensely in preconvention activities. He chose or accepted a campaign staff and organized it along the military lines to which he was accustomed; he established campaign headquarters in Denver; he made speeches in several states; and he met with delegation after delegation and with representatives of special interest groups.

Meanwhile, his astute political managers, Lodge, Herbert Brownell, and Sherman Adams, set about convincing Republican regulars in various ways, some of them fairly ruthless, that a sentimental attachment to Taft and strict conservatism must not be allowed to prevent an election victory and that only under Eisenhower's banner could the Republicans, after twenty years of denial, win the White House that year. They drafted a convention rules-change that they dubbed the "Fair Play Amendment" whereby no contested delegate who had been temporarily seated could vote to seat himself permanently (or to seat any other contested delegate permanently) unless he had first received two-thirds of the vote of the National Committee to confirm his temporary status. Such a majority was larger than the Taft forces controlled. A floor strategy was worked out for securing adoption of this amendment and for handling Eisenhower's candidacy thereafter. When Eisenhower himself arrived in Chicago, the convention city, on July 5, Lodge and Brownell saw to it that delegates who complained they had not met him and did not know what he stood for were run through his Blackstone Hotel suite on a rigid time-schedule from morning to late at night. The last delegation, Eisenhower wrote in his book *Mandate For Change*, left from its visit "only an hour before the balloting for the nomination was scheduled to begin."

By that time there was no doubt in Eisenhower's mind what the outcome would be. The Fair Play Amendment had been adopted, and the vote for it indicated Eisenhower's strength. At the end of

The Nixons and Eisenhowers acknowledge victory at the Convention.

REPUBLICAN NAT

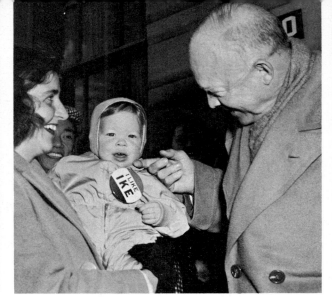

the first ballot, Eisenhower had 595 votes (nine short of victory) to Taft's 500. Then, the leader of the Minnesota delegation called for the floor and announced that Minnesota, whose earlier vote had gone to favorite son Harold Stassen, wished to switch to Eisenhower. That clinched it; the General was the Republican nominee. A short while later, the convention nominated his personal choice for Vice President, Richard M. Nixon. That evening, Eisenhower delivered his acceptance speech, saying he was heeding a call to lead a "crusade for freedom in America and freedom in the world. . . ." From that moment on, by his own account, he felt no "doubt, other than in fleeting moments, as to the November outcome."

Nevertheless, he waged an arduous campaign. At its outset, hopes were high for an elevated national dialogue on crucial public issues. Two weeks after Eisenhower's nomination, in that same Chicago amphitheatre where he had triumphed, Governor Adlai E. Stevenson of Illinois delivered his acceptance speech of the Democratic nomination. "The ordeal of the twentieth century—the bloodiest, most turbulent era of the Christian age—is far from over," said Stevenson. "Let's face it! Let's talk sense to the American people!" Stevenson's attempt to do so was enlivened by an eloquence and wit unprecedented in American politics. Eisenhower's speeches proved to be of a different order. They were notably solemn as they exploited to the full the issues of Korea, corruption, and Communism in government. "It would be very, very fine if one could command new and amusing language," said Eisenhower, "witticisms to bring you a chuckle. Frankly, I have no intention of trying to do so. The subjects of which we are speaking these days . . . are not those that seem to me to be amusing. . . ."

Many of his most ardent Republican supporters had hoped and believed he would liberalize his party, but his campaign did little toward this end. In the second week of September, he had a much publicized peacemaking meeting with Taft, issuing with Taft a joint statement prepared by the latter in which Eisenhower seemed to concede every point of difference between Republican liberals and Taft's Old Guard. He did not dissociate himself in any publicly effective way from McCarthy and McCarthyism. On the contrary, he permitted himself to be embraced physically as well as figuratively by the man who had called Marshall a "living lie," Indiana's Senator Jenner, for whose re-election he called in glowing words. He then gave rather more than tacit support to McCarthy's re-election (which was then far from certain) by saying that he and the Senator agreed on "ends," differing only on "methods."

The most dismaying episode of the campaign, as far as he personally was concerned, was a seemingly dangerous backfiring of the corruption issue when newsmen discovered that Nixon had been given a large sum of money by a group of California businessmen so that he could "afford" to engage in politics. The fright among Republicans was great but short-lived. Nixon went before TV cameras in a broadcast seen by some sixty million people, bared his finances and his soul to the American people, and emerged with his vote-getting appeal not merely unscathed but actually enhanced. Eisenhower watched the telecast in the office of the manager of the Cleveland Public Auditorium. He was tre-

Opposite: A vigorous campaigner, Eisenhower tries out new headgear, greets two of his youngest fans, waves to a crowd in Indiana with Chief Lone Eagle, and accepts an eighty-pound pumpkin in Minnesota. Above, weary from all the stumping, he takes a cat nap on his campaign airplane.

Confident of victory, Ike greets an audience, below, on election eve, 1952, with his "V" sign. The next day (as shown above) he carried all but nine states.

mendously moved. "I like courage," he told a huge Cleveland audience that night. "Tonight I saw an example of courage."

As regards Korea, Eisenhower said that if there must be war in Asia "let it be Asians against Asians"; that Americans in the future "must avoid the kind of bungling that led us into Korea . . ."; and, in late October, barely a week before the election, that if elected he would "go to Korea" to seek "an early and honorable" end to the war there. By his own account, he had been considering for some time the advisability of his visiting Korea, if he was elected, but the idea of publicly announcing his decision to do so was given him by C. D. Jackson of Time, Inc., one of his staff advisers. ". . . I replied . . . 'You're a great man, C. D., you agree with me.' However, there was a difference: my feeling about the idea was the need for making the trip if elected; his was on the effect a public announcement of the intention would have on the election."

There is no doubt that the Korean promise swelled the size of Eisenhower's election victory. An unprecedented total of 61,250,000 votes were cast on November 4, 1952, and of these Eisenhower won approximately 34,000,000, carrying all but nine states (he carried four in the South), to gain 442 electoral votes to Stevenson's 89. But the margin of this victory was great enough to show that Eisenhower would almost certainly have won handily even without his promise to go to Korea.

In retrospect it seems clear that so far as the decisive independent vote was concerned, the election contest that year was not between two living men, two actual minds and characters, but between two animated images. Stevenson was depicted by most of the press as an "egghead" (the term was coined that year), an intellectual who was glib and witty, amusing at times, but not to be taken seriously as an administrator of large practical affairs. Eisenhower, on the other hand, was "Ike" of the wide grin whom everybody liked —not a show-off or smart aleck but a wise, compassionate man, profoundly good in the moral sense, with a proved ability to administer huge enterprises of crucial importance. On the troubled national scene, he was a soothing figure. The "Ike" image was to a large degree a projection of Eisenhower's own view of himself, as the words he spoke were to a large degree expressive of his own attitudes and opinions. He really believed that most of America's troubles were manufactured by Left Wingers who were ambitious for the power of centralized government. He really was contemptuous of eggheads, with their fancy theories, and convinced of the superiority of his own hard practical common sense.

This combination of factors or forces, joined to the public's profound wish to believe in Eisenhower and all he stood for, produced a political popularity remarkable for potency and longevity. It survived the vicissitudes of four years in the White House. Perhaps it would have been reduced if the Republicans had retained control of Congress in the mid-term elections of 1954; Eisenhower might then have become identified with the unpopular policies of his party. But the Democrats won that year; the public refused to regard this as a repudiation of Eisenhower's personal leadership.

Then on the night of Friday, September 23, 1955, Eisenhower, on vacation in Denver, having played golf most of the day, suffered

President-elect Eisenhower balances a plate on his knees in an Army chow line, after keeping a campaign promise to go to Korea.

107

a severe heart attack. He was bedridden for weeks and convalesced for many weeks thereafter. He emerged from his ordeal more beloved of the populace than before, his political appeal actually increased as his doctors assured the public that he was perfectly fit to run for re-election. Nor was his appeal at all reduced when, on June 8, 1956, he was struck down by his second dangerous illness in nine months. He underwent emergency surgery on the morning of June 9 to relieve obstruction of the ileum. Barely eleven hours after this surgery began, the doctor who performed it told a jam-packed press conference that there was no medical reason why Eisenhower should not run for re-election, that "rapid and complete recovery" was expected, that the President should be able to resume the "full duties" of his office in four to six weeks, and that he would be playing golf again in mid-August.

On the morrow of the heart attack, everyone assumed that the President could not run again. The Democratic nomination, which would otherwise have gone to Stevenson virtually uncontested, became suddenly a prize worth fighting for. Governor Averell Harriman of New York announced his candidacy. So did Senator Estes Kefauver of Tennessee. Stevenson was forced into a bitter primary battle with Kefauver from which Stevenson emerged victorious but exhausted and with the image he personally had projected in 1952 badly tarnished. He had no real chance against Eisenhower in the campaign that followed. His defeat was more overwhelming than that of 1952. Eisenhower carried forty-one of the forty-eight states, winning 457 electoral votes compared to Stevenson's 74. His popular vote was 35,582,236 as compared to Stevenson's 26,028,887.

Nor was Eisenhower's political popularity perceptibly reduced by his second term in the White House. Indeed, his decisive action in sending Federal troops into Little Rock, Arkansas, in 1957, to enforce a Federal court's ruling on integration won him increased respect. And, in July of 1958, when the Sixth Fleet and some 9,000 Marines were sent to counter the threat against Lebanon by Egypt and Syria, Eisenhower again emerged as a forceful leader in the view of many critics. But, these were years of rapid and momentous change in world affairs. A chaotic world revolution proceeded apace as formerly colonial peoples, having stagnated for centuries in the most primitive economies, increasingly absorbed Western technology and (alas) an outmoded Western nationalism. Every scale of value by which world-political judgments must be measured was drastically altered; each year as nuclear weaponry became more widely spread, the ultimate issue of world government or world destruction presented itself more starkly. To these immense challenges, the Eisenhower Administration made, in the opinion of such contemporary historians as Henry Steele Commager, inadequate response. Yet the affection the American people felt for Ike continued. Few among his friends or foes had the slightest doubt that, had the law permitted and had he desired it, he could again have been elected President by a huge majority in 1960.

Obviously, this smiling, likable man who had come from a humble home in a country town to the highest office of a highly urbanized America stood for something immensely precious to the great bulk of his countrymen.

Hail to the Chief

Chief Justice Earl Warren administers the oath of office to Eisenhower, officially marking the beginning of his second term as President. Richard Nixon, to the President's right, waits to be sworn in for his second term as Vice President. Mamie Eisenhower watches the ceremonies from the front row (far left) along with Former President Herbert Hoover, third from the left in the front row.

OVERLEAF: *A panoramic view of Capitol Hill taken from nearby the Supreme Court building shows the crowd gathered in front of the east steps of the Capitol for Eisenhower's inaugural ceremonies.*

*President and Mrs. Eisenhower happily applaud the festivities at one of
the four balls held in their honor after the 1957 inauguration. During the hectic
evening the Eisenhowers put in an appearance at each of the balls.*

Ike as President

by RICHARD M. NIXON

As Vice President during Eisenhower's Administration, Richard M. Nixon was particularly close to the President, both officially and personally. In the following selection from his book Six Crises,* *published in 1962, Mr. Nixon reveals some of Eisenhower's personal characteristics.*

. . . as I went to see Eisenhower [on September 15, 1952] the road ahead seemed full of promise and no pitfalls. . . . I saw General Eisenhower that evening in his headquarters at the Brown Palace Hotel in Denver. The place was swarming with aides, party workers, and visiting dignitaries. It had the aura of a command post. Eisenhower was not the ordinary run-of-the-mill candidate seeking friends and supporters. He had been Commander of all Allied troops in Europe during the Second World War; he was the General who won the war; and even as a candidate he was accorded the respect, honor, and awe that only a President usually receives. Despite his great capacity for friendliness, he also had a quality of reserve which, at least subconsciously, tended to make a visitor feel like a junior officer coming in to see the commanding General.

The first time I ever saw Eisenhower, he was in fact the victorious commanding General. It was shortly after V-E Day. I was thirty-two years old and a Lieutenant Commander in the Navy. After returning from service overseas in the South Pacific, I was assigned the task of negotiating settlements of terminated war contracts in the Bureau of Aeronautics Office at 50 Church Street, New York City. General Eisenhower, the returning hero, was riding through the streets of Manhattan in the greatest ticker-tape parade in the city's history. As I looked down from a twentieth floor window, I could see him standing in the back of his car with both arms raised high over his head. It was a gesture which was to become his political trademark in the years ahead.

I met him again five years later at the Bohemian Grove, near San Francisco, where we were both luncheon guests of former President Herbert Hoover. I had just won the Republican nomination for the United States Senate in California. We were introduced, but he met so many others during his stay there that I doubted then if he would remember me.

Less than a year later, in December of 1951, I met him again at the Headquarters of SHAPE in Paris, and this time we talked for almost forty-five minutes. He made a great impression on me with his grasp of international affairs. I came away from that meeting with my first personal understanding of the Eisenhower popularity: he had an incomparable ability to show a deep interest in a wide range of subjects, and he displayed as much interest when he listened as when he spoke. I recall that he was particularly interested in my role in the Hiss case. He had read accounts of it and pointed out that one of the reasons I had been successful where others in the Communist investigating field had failed was that I had insisted on scrupulously fair procedures in my handling of the case.

In Denver that Monday night we reviewed our campaign strategy. The plan was for General Eisenhower to stress the positive aspects of his "Crusade to Clean Up the Mess in Washington." I was to hammer away at our opponents on the record of the Truman Administration, with particular emphasis on Communist subversion because of my work in the Hiss case.

I left Denver early the next morning ready for battle and confident of victory. . . .

Stripped of all personal and collateral considerations, the real issue was: who would win the election, Eisenhower or Stevenson? To me, this was not a choice between two equally able men who happened to be members of different parties. I will admit that I was not an objective observer; but to me Eisenhower was a great leader who could provide the inspiration needed by the United States and the Free World in so critical a time. . . .

* * *

On Saturday, September 24, 1955, the United States Senate was not in session, and any concern about the state of the President's health was the furthest thing from my mind. . . .

I . . . was checking the baseball averages in the sports section when the phone rang. I walked into the hall and picked up the receiver. "Dick," said a familiar voice, "this is Jim Hagerty—the President has had a coronary."

It is impossible to describe how I felt when I heard these words. The news was so unexpected, the shock so great that I could think of nothing to say for several seconds. . . .

I had been completely unprepared for this turn of events. During the three years I had been Vice President, there had never been any reason to worry about the President's health. He had waged a vigorous campaign in 1952, and since his inauguration, despite newspaper criticism of his vacations and his golf, he had maintained a strict schedule of early rising and hard work at his desk. He was, in fact, a superb specimen of a man who believed in keeping himself physically fit. Golf was part of the regimen prescribed by his doctor as the best means of relieving the tremendous tension and strain of the presidency. . . .

The personal crisis for Dwight D. Eisenhower was not the heart attack per se, because he had no control over that, but the decision of whether or not, after such a brush with death,

*Six Crises © 1962 BY RICHARD M. NIXON, REPRINTED BY PERMISSION OF DOUBLEDAY & COMPANY, INC.

to run for re-election in 1956. The basic considerations which went into this decision were the same before and after September 1955—with the exception of the heart attack—and I believe it was the heart attack itself which, more than anything else, helped convince him to become a candidate for re-election.

Eisenhower frequently had told his associates that he wanted to be a one-term President. He thought that in four years he could substitute his concept of a moderate federal government, a free economy, and a balanced budget for what he considered the Democratic Party's drift toward a welfare state. He wanted to build up the Republican Party into a moderate, responsible majority party, and then turn over the reins to a younger man. He intended to put this concept of a one-term President into his first inaugural address, but at the last minute he was talked out of that. However, this did not stop him from discussing the idea. . . .

He was not in office much more than a year when he began to tell associates from time to time of his intention to retire at the end of his first term. Usually these outbursts were recognized as temporary sentiments of the moment, reflecting a recent setback of one kind or another. But as 1956 approached, they were regarded more and more seriously.

When he moved his office to Denver, August 14, 1955, the political pressures on the President to run again in 1956 had reached a crescendo. The Republican National Convention was just a year off. The respite from urgent government business at Denver was seen as a time when the President could reach the all-important political decision on a second term. At Denver, before the heart attack, Eisenhower seemed particularly testy, easily irritated, and on edge. He kept putting off those who wanted to talk politics with the exclamation that he was in Denver to fish and play golf.

Two weeks before the heart attack, following a meeting of Republican State Chairmen, Len Hall visited Eisenhower in Denver to press upon him the party's and the nation's need for him to run for re-election. The President listened and paced the floor, and told the party Chairman what he had told others: "What more do they want from me? . . . I've given all of my adult life to the country. . . . What more must I do? . . ." He then went on to list five or six names, mine included, of men he said were younger than he and just as able to carry on the Eisenhower mode of government.

Hall left that meeting discouraged, but not convinced that the chances of Eisenhower's running were hopeless. Hagerty, Adams, myself, and others in the Administration had heard the President speak of retirement, but we knew that the nature of the office always leaves important unfinished business at the end of a President's term of office, and that few real leaders can turn their backs on such a challenge. We knew that Eisen-

hower was not a quitter—that he liked to finish a job which he had started. Our arguments to him stressed that he was the best if not the only man who could accomplish the undone work which lay ahead.

If I had bet at that time, I would have wagered that he would seek a second term. Incidentally, my judgment of what Eisenhower would do was not based on any theory that a man in power loves power for its own sake. The office of President of the United States carries an aura of responsibility which transcends the personal power the office holds. It demands a dedication and devotion which is greater than any personal consideration of the man who occupies the office. No leader of men who has occupied that office and devoted his being to it can turn away when his work is still incomplete. To a lesser extent this holds true for leaders in other walks of life, who carry on despite great financial and physical problems. . . .

Eisenhower demonstrated a trait that I believe all great

leaders have in common: they thrive on challenge; they are at their best when the going is hardest. When life is routine, they become bored; when they have no challenge, they tend to wither and die or to go to seed. While such men might think and often exclaim how nice it would be if they could play golf every day and take long vacations whenever they wished, in actual fact they need challenges, problems, and hard work to sustain the will to live.

Commander in Chief

by ADMIRAL ARTHUR W. RADFORD

Admiral Arthur W. Radford, Chairman of the Joint Chiefs of Staff during most of Eisenhower's first term as President, took a leading role in shaping the defense policies of the Eisenhower Administration. Here he writes of the close professional, and personal, relationship he had with the President.

Any man who has been elected and re-elected as President of the United States is bound to have left his mark on the history of the world. With considerable prejudice in President Eisenhower's favor—for I served as his Chairman of the Joint Chiefs of Staff for four years—I wish to tell the story of what history may record as his most important decision.

I could well start by going back to 1917 and the Bolshevik revolution, when the Communists took over the government in Russia and started the buildup of what has become in our day a monolithic military power, and then relate how in the years between 1917 and 1965, with intervals of setbacks and internal trouble, communism continued to grow in influence.

I choose to start my story in May of 1953—on the evening of the fifteenth to be exact—at Pearl Harbor, Hawaii, where I was stationed at the time as Commander in Chief of the Pacific Command. That evening the late Assistant Secretary of Defense Frank Nash stopped at Honolulu en route to the Far East. Secretary Nash, a close and warm friend, was my house guest. When I met him he took me aside and informed me that at about seven o'clock the next morning my telephone at home would start to ring because newsmen in Honolulu would want comments from the next Chairman of the Joint Chiefs of Staff. He explained that at noon the next day, Washington time, the White House was to announce that the President was nominating me as Chairman of the Joint Chiefs of Staff to succeed General Bradley. This would be seven A.M. Hawaiian time, and I could expect to be called first by local newsmen who would see it on the ticker. To my complete surprise he turned out to be right. Confirmation accomplished, I was ordered to Washington, after being relieved of my command at Pearl Harbor, and I arrived in the Capital on July 15.

I found other new members of the Joint Chiefs of Staff already in Washington: General Twining, Admiral Carney, and General Ridgway. I called on President Eisenhower as soon as he could see me. I had seen General Eisenhower only once, and then briefly, since the time he had served as Chief of Staff of the Army in President Truman's Administration—the time, indeed, when I happened to be opposing his plans for the unification of the services. At our first meeting the President

asked me whether I would like to see him every Monday morning at nine thirty. I told him I did not know what demands there would be in my new position and whether or not I would have anything to talk to him about. "That's all right," the President said. "If you don't have anything to talk about, maybe I will. Then, if something comes up, I can usually save it for a week—and, if you are coming here regularly, no particular attention will be drawn to your visits." I recall many times, in those weekly meetings, when the President would ask me if I had anything to discuss, and if I had not, he would pace around the room and talk about whatever came to his mind.

In our first several meetings, the President outlined in considerable detail what he wanted me to do in the interval before I took over. He said that historically the military forces in the United States had experienced either a feast or a famine. Faced with a crisis, nothing was too good for them. Postwar, the economizers took over, and our regular military establish-

ment withered on the vine until the next crisis occurred. He traced the history of the last three of our wars, and said he doubted that any one of them would have been fought if the United States had had, before the war started, an adequate military posture—well-balanced Army-Navy forces in being, known to be well trained and well equipped. As President he had decided, he said, that with the settlement of the Korean War he was not again going to enfeeble our armed strength.

He felt that the world situation required balanced United States armed forces that were strong enough to deter a challenge by any nation and particularly by the Soviet Union.

He directed that the new Chiefs of Staff meet together, without staff assistance, and work up in outline the military structure we thought the country should have to insure the peace he envisaged. Traditionally, he told the chiefs, military men were supposedly concerned only with the force requirements—not costs. While he was not putting a ceiling on costs, he wanted us as chiefs to look at our total national strength in connection with our planning, economic as well as military. He was thinking in such long-range terms—twenty, forty, fifty years, as long as the threat to peace remained—that obviously our total expenditures had to bear a satisfactory relationship to total income over the whole time period. He wanted a "pay-as-you-go" system if it were at all possible. He reasoned that it was essential that our allies have confidence in the long-range fiscal policies of this country as well as in its military strength. Such confidence was further necessary because he wanted allied military forces included in the free world strength. We would help those who needed help to generate military forces which in turn would reduce some of our own requirements.

In order that we could be alone to work out a plan, the new Chiefs boarded the Secretary of the Navy's yacht on the Potomac in early August. A draft was given to the President that same month, and by the end of August the basis of what later was to be called the New Look had been approved by the President after favorable consideration by the National Security Council. Later that fall the Joint Chiefs of Staff appointed a special committee to work up a detailed force structure; costs were estimated to be in the thirty-three to thirty-five billion range for new money in each fiscal year. It was a far cry from the ten- to twelve-billion limit of post World War II, which left our defenses so dangerously weakened and, undoubtedly, encouraged the Communists to enter Korea in 1950 with the expectation of victory.

A defense appropriation of this magnitude for the indefinite future was unheard of in the history of our country. Only a strong President would dare to commit himself and his party to such a program.

This was the fall of 1953. In every year since then, the defense appropriation has approximated 50 per cent or more of the national budget. Unquestionably, the military strength of the United States has prevented World War III and has so far maintained the confidence of our allies. The courage and foresight of a President with a military background stabilized a world situation that the Communists hoped for a while they could control. We must pray that President Eisenhower's successors will be as wise as he, and as courageous.

Ike on a Red Carpet

During the last two years of his administration, anxious to bolster America's "image" in the face of the Soviet Union's successes in space, President Eisenhower embarked on a series of six international good-will trips. He traveled 320,000 miles and stopped off at twenty-seven countries. He visited cities most Americans had never heard of; he was showered with chrysanthemums and kissed by priestesses; he waved to and beamed at millions of people who waved back and cheered him on. Most of the traveling was done by jet, and Eisenhower seldom lingered in any country for more than three days. Sometimes, as in Afghanistan, he stayed less than two hours. While the schedules exhausted his aides, Eisenhower's enthusiasm only grew. No matters of state were resolved by the President's travels. Yet, he opened up a broad area of personal diplomacy that helped nurture international understanding at its simplest, and its most vitally important, level. The reception accorded him in 1960 in Rio de Janeiro (right) was typical: Brazil's flamboyant President, Juscelino Kubitschek, greeting Eisenhower at right, ordered a 105-gun salute for the American leader.

Above, President Eisenhower and Pope John XXIII trade jokes in Vatican City.   *Brazilians (above) and Formosans (opposite) cheer Ike.*

Ike is met by the Shah (above) as Iranians prepare a welcome (right). Below, Ike visits Nehru.

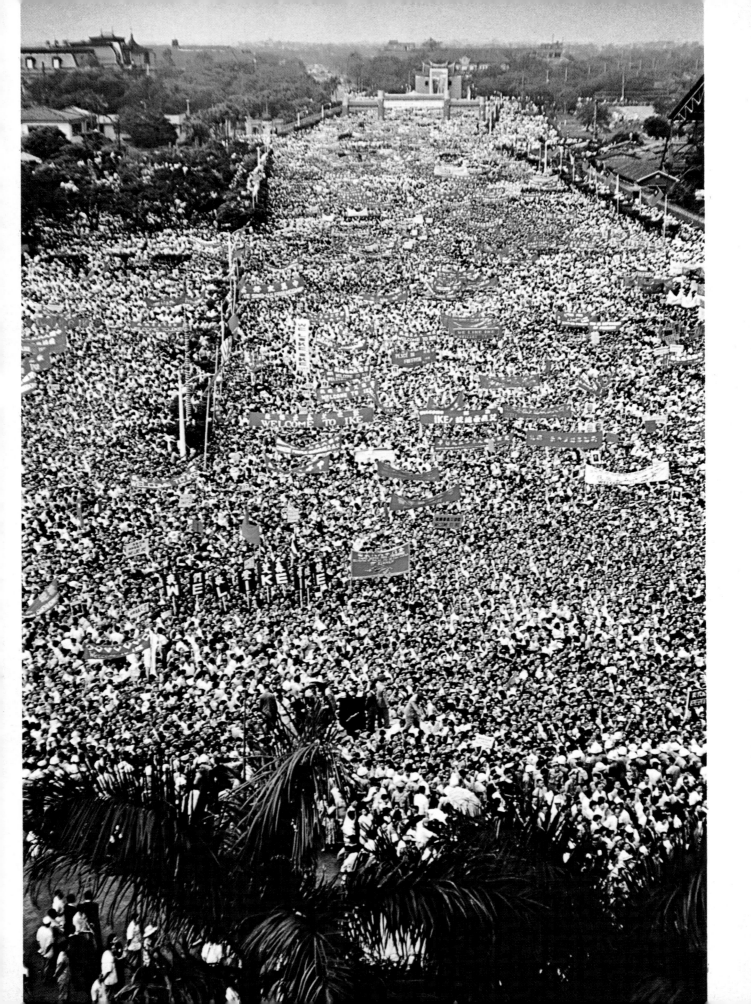

*President Eisenhower fields a question
at his weekly press conference, at right.
Below, with the same care and gusto, he
performs another official function:
opening the American League baseball
season at Washington's Griffith Stadium.*

VI

MR. PRESIDENT

On January 19, 1953, the eve of his first inauguration as President of the United States, Dwight Eisenhower sought to draw strength for the future from his roots in the past. At a family reunion with his four brothers and their wives in Washington's Statler Hotel, he paid in spirit a nostalgic visit to Abilene. The dry prose of his memoirs gives a bare hint of his emotions: ". . . we were able to get together and reminisce," he writes, adding that "a highlight" of the whole historic occasion for him "was the dinner we all had together on my final evening as a private citizen."

He may be pictured at that dinner, seated at the head of the table, his mobile countenance reflecting in swift succession his various moods as all the brothers recalled incidents of the old days in the Kansas country town—the time Edgar and he forgot to deliver their father's lunch and were punished for it by their mother as never before or after; the time he had knocked out Dirk Tyler in a boxing match; the hours of hard work in the family garden; and the hours they had fidgeted and squirmed through seemingly endless Bible readings at home and sermons at church. He could not but feel a sense of wonder, of awe, as he looked back over the long way that had brought him from Abilene to his present position. "There had been dramatic events in my life before—but none surpassed, emotionally, crossing the threshold to an office of such awesome responsibility," he wrote later. "Remembering my beginnings, I had to smile. . . . the . . . old saw had proved to be true: in the United States, any boy *can* grow up to be President."

The phrase "any boy" is revealing. In his own view, as in those of his brothers and others who had known him when he was growing up, Dwight Eisenhower remained in essential respects the boy he had been in Abilene. He had "matured early," as the saying goes. When he left Abilene for West Point on a June day in 1911, his mind had been stocked with mid-nineteenth century ideas regarding economic individualism, the proper role of government in a democracy, and the nature of human freedom. He was of the same mind still. His personal tastes and interests and attitudes were also much the same: his passion for competitive games was undiminished, golf and bridge being substitutes for the team sports of his Abilene years; his favorite reading for relaxation continued to be Wild Western pulp magazines; and now no more than then was he inclined to put on airs or set himself apart as superior to ordinary people. He was in many ways profoundly humble, presenting far less egoistic resistance to the wishes of others than most men (certainly most in his position) would have done.

His chief pride, or his greatest self-confidence, lay in his ability to get people to cooperate with one another toward common goals. He was himself so little moved by power lusts that he could not really understand men of very different temper and motives. Hence his conviction that his personality and conciliatory talents would cause men who were gathered around a table under his chairmanship to arrive at a working consensus, no matter how violent their initial disagreements. He would preside; they, as a group, would decide. Seldom, and then with extreme reluctance, would he exercise his own decisive will. Significant in this connection is the closing sentence of the short prayer with which, on January 20, he preceded his inaugural address. With Mamie he had attended services in Washington's National Presbyterian Church that morning. He had but lately (since his election victory) become a church member for the first time in his adult life. "Religion," he says in his memoirs, "was one of the thoughts I had been mulling over for several weeks." And on the way back to the hotel from church he was suddenly inspired to open his Presidency with a prayer, which he promptly wrote out. "May cooperation be permitted and be the mutual aim of those who, under the concepts of our Constitution, hold to different political faiths," he said, "so that all may work for the good of our beloved country and Thy glory. Amen."

Occupied by a man of these qualities and beliefs, the office of the Presidency was a far less potent one than it had been under Truman or Roosevelt or even Hoover. America was embarked on another experiment in congressional government, its nature and dangers enhanced and dramatized in 1953–54 by the active presence in the Senate of Joseph McCarthy.

As chairman of the Permanent Investigations Subcommittee of the Senate Committee on Governmental Operations, McCarthy disrupted one Executive agency after another, destroyed one career of public service after another with wild but hugely headlined charges of "Communist subversive" or "fellow traveler" hurled at men of liberal views or, often, at men who merely happened to have annoyed the senator or questioned his motives or methods. Immense harm was done the United States' foreign relations. The opinion of many observers was that the constitutional division of powers among the Executive, the Legislative, and the Judicial branches implied an obligation upon the Chief Executive to protect his office and its active authority against such a flagrant abuse of congressional investigative rights and procedures. Moreover, most knowledgeable observers were convinced that the President had only to issue an unequivocal condemnation of McCarthy and McCarthyism to do the job. Eisenhower disagreed. Such action "would greatly enhance . . . [McCarthy's] publicity value without achieving any constructive purpose," he later wrote. (To intimates he reportedly said, "I will not get down in the gutter with that guy.") McCarthy, he insisted, would eventually "destroy himself."

Above, Senator Joseph McCarthy testifies at the Senate "Army-McCarthy" hearings, 1954. G. David Schine (center) confers with Roy Cohn.

Federal troops quell a disturbance over integration in Birmingham, above, in 1957. Below, John Foster Dulles works at the U.N. during the Suez crisis.

And finally, McCarthy *did* overreach himself. He attacked the U.S. Army (Communists had infiltrated the armed services, he said) and over-exposed his personality and methods in a prolonged, nationally televised hearing. At last, on December 2, 1954, by a vote of sixty-seven to twenty-two, the Senate formally condemned McCarthy for conduct "contrary to senatorial traditions." This marked the end of the Wisconsin senator's reign of terror.

Eisenhower was more active in his opposition to Republican Senator John Bricker's proposal to limit the treaty-making power of the President and the Senate by a constitutional amendment saying that a treaty could "become effective as internal law . . . only through legislation which would be valid in the absence of a treaty." If adopted, the amendment with its "which" clause would make it impossible for the Executive to conduct foreign affairs, Eisenhower protested—and in late February, 1954, after long debate, the proposal failed by a single vote to obtain the two-thirds majority of the Senate required for passage.

It could be expected that a President of Eisenhower's temperament, theories of government, and Army staff-experience would make larger delegations of his authority to subordinates than most Presidents had done—and in the event, these delegations were of unprecedented size and quality. Sherman Adams, the former New Hampshire governor who bore the title of Assistant to the President, became in actual operation a deputy-President who (as he privately said) did whatever needed to be done that the President himself did not do. Adams was a taciturn man of peculiarly graceless manners who was cordially disliked by leading members of Congress. Few in Washington were grief-stricken when disclosure that he had accepted favors from a New England industrialist forced his resignation just prior to the 1958 elections. Press Secretary James Hagerty, on the other hand, was generally popular. His public relations sense and his genius for news management were exercised within far wider limits of discretion than are commonly alloted White House spokesmen. Vice President Nixon, too, exerted far more influence upon policy and far more executive authority than normally pertains to the office he occupied. It was he who did most to settle the prolonged steel strike of 1959, personally intervening in negotiations between management and labor; of all the top echelon of the Administration he pressed hardest for government actions to end recessions and promote prosperity; and he not infrequently dealt influentially with foreign relations. But the two strong men of the Administration, largely responsible for its record in domestic and foreign affairs, were Secretary of the Treasury George M. Humphrey and Secretary of State John Foster Dulles.

Humphrey, who had had much the same kind of Midwestern, small-town boyhood as Eisenhower and who was almost precisely Eisenhower's age, had as top executive of the huge M. A. Hanna Company in Cleveland acquired a fortune of many millions. He was a man of great personal force and charm who became a fast friend of the President's. Humphrey was also a man of rigidly orthodox conservative economic views, suspicious of the activities of government regulatory agencies, convinced that high taxes and big government spending were destroying private enterprise. He

123

was equally convinced that America's moral nature was being corrupted by the increasingly large part the government had been taking in economic affairs. As candidate, Eisenhower had stressed the need for "sound fiscal practices" and for avoiding "further deterioration in the value of our currency"; as President, he was receptive of Humphrey's proposals for curbing inflation, the greatest of all long-term threats, in Humphrey's profound belief.

The Administration therefore pursued in general a tight-money policy and pressed hard for government economies that would ultimately bring about a balanced budget and a cut in taxes. A consequence of this policy, according to Administration critics, was a lowered over-all rate of economic growth and a series of recessions, some of them severe, during the eight Eisenhower years. All government agencies felt the effects of this pressure for reduced spending, but the greatest political outcry was provoked by heavy cuts made in defense appropriations—notably a five billion cut in Air Force appropriations approved by Eisenhower in the spring of 1953. Eisenhower's Secretary of Defense, Charles E. Wilson, a former head of General Motors, thoroughly agreed with Humphrey's economic philosophy and was sure that by eliminating waste and duplication, great reduction in defense costs could be achieved without impairment of the nation's armed strength. "More bang for a buck" became a motto of the Republicans. And this of course had direct implications for foreign policy, as conducted by Secretary of State Dulles.

Dulles, a hugely successful corporation lawyer, the grandson of one former Secretary of State and the nephew of another, had all his adult life been preparing to become Secretary of State in a Republican administration. He had had extensive experience with foreign affairs, dating back to the 1907 peace conference at The Hague where, at age nineteen, he had been secretary to the Chinese delegation. He was a religious man, one of the lay leaders of the Presbyterian Church, inclined to couch his pronouncements in moralistic terms. He had little of Humphrey's (or Eisenhower's) personal likableness; but he had a swift, wide-ranging, well-informed mind, and Eisenhower regarded him as "the greatest Secretary of State in history." Certainly Dulles exercised the greatest policy-making authority of any Secretary of State in history.

In January, 1954, in an address to the Council on Foreign Relations, Dulles announced that the United States would no longer rely on the "traditional" policy of "meeting aggression by direct and local oppositions" but would instead "depend primarily upon a great capacity to retaliate instantly, by means and at places of our choosing." This was the doctrine of massive retaliation, which was consistent with, if not actually determined by, the Administration's economic policies. As America's strength in conventional arms was reduced, increased reliance would be placed upon atomic weapons. In January, 1956, in an article in *Life* Magazine, Dulles described the art of diplomacy as consisting in part of the ability to go to the brink of war without toppling over. This was the much-controverted doctrine of "brinkmanship," expressive of Dulles' deep feeling that only the language of fear and force could be effective in dealing with Soviet Russia. Others of his statements further

Eisenhower was up and around quickly after his heart attack on September 24, 1955. For his first appearance outside the hospital, above, his pajamas bore the response, "Much Better Thanks." Opposite, several months later, Ike takes to the golf course outside Thomasville, Georgia.

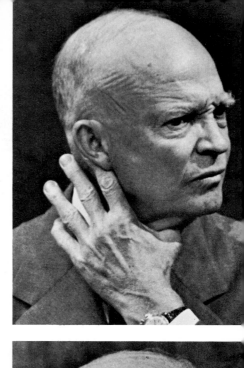

Eisenhower initiated the television press conference,
and he clearly enjoyed his weekly sessions. His face was
mobile and eminently expressive as he put a hand up
to his ear to listen to a question, as he pondered
a reporter's remarks, and as he responded—sometimes
somberly, sometimes angrily, sometimes with a sheepish
grin. Above, in the midst of a prepared statement,
he removes his glasses to laugh at a reporter's barb.

revealed his belief that negotiations with Communist states were not only futile but wrong: since communism was inherently evil, agreement with it was a compromise with wickedness.

These doctrines, these personal feelings and beliefs, determined the conduct of America's foreign affairs during the two Eisenhower terms. There were numerous "brinks": increased Communist aggressions against the Chinese Nationalist islands of Quemoy and Matsu, whose defense was linked with that of Formosa and, according to many observers, with the defense of much of the Far East; repeated Berlin crises; the French loss of Indochina to rebellious colonials despite American aid; the Suez crisis; direct U.S. intervention against Communists in Lebanon; the Soviet capture of an American U-2 reconnaissance plane deep in Russian territory, resulting in the collapse of a Paris summit meeting. There were moments of relaxed tension, even brief surges of hope for permanent settlements, but in general the mutually hostile postures of the United States and Soviet Russia seemed frozen into absolute rigidity as Eisenhower's second term came to an end.

In reviewing Eisenhower's Presidency, some historians have listed his handling of the Little Rock crisis over integration and his farewell address warning of the dangers of a vast military-industrial complex as belonging among his major achievements. Others, while mindful of the uneasiness Americans felt about the "brink" approached during the Suez crisis, have praised his diplomatic maneuvers in resolving that difficult situation. Yet, Eisenhower himself may well have felt that one of his greatest moments came in 1957 with the establishment of an International Atomic Energy Agency as part of the United Nations organization. The initiating idea had been Eisenhower's own. In early 1953, as he later wrote in a letter to a friend, he "began to search . . . for . . . an idea that could bring the world to look at the atomic problem in a broad and intelligent way and still escape the impasse . . . created by Russian intransigence in the matter of mutual or neutral inspection of resources." The idea he finally "hit upon" was that "of actual physical donations of [uranium] isotopes . . . to a common fund for peaceful purposes," which meant not only donations from America's "then unequalled nuclear stockpile" but also donations from Soviet Russia and Britain.

On December 8, 1953, presenting the idea in a speech ("Atoms for Peace") to the United Nations General Assembly, Eisenhower stated: "Against the dark background of the atomic bomb, the United States does not wish merely to present strength, but also the desire and the hope for peace . . . the United States pledges before you—and therefore before the world—its determination to help solve the fearful atomic dilemma—to devote its entire heart and mind to find the way by which the miraculous inventiveness of man shall not be dedicated to his death, but consecrated to his life. . . ."

Here, one feels, in these words addressed to an organization Eisenhower felt to be the hope for world peace, is the essential Eisenhower, as he wished throughout his life to be—the selfless nonpartisan hero, the symbol of the unity of mankind, a leader toward that world order which is so clearly necessary if a civilized human freedom is to survive.

Eisenhower turned over his office to President John F. Kennedy in 1961 and, with Mamie, he retired to his farm in Gettysburg (opposite). Although he continued to be called upon for advice (above, he strolls with Kennedy at Camp David at the time of the Cuban missile crisis), 1961 marked, for him, the formal end of fifty years of public service.

The Final Years

When Eisenhower retired, the nomadic habit of half a century of public life remained with him. "Home" became the farmhouse in Gettysburg that he had built while he was President; a four-bedroom rented cottage on the grounds of the elegant Eldorado Country Club near Palm Springs, California; and a little white frame house near the Augusta, Georgia, National Golf Course.

Finally out of the limelight, Eisenhower worked on his memoirs in an office at Gettysburg College and relaxed at the farm. Augusta was for golf, but the Eisenhowers went there less often than to the Eldorado, where they spent an average of four months each winter. There he occasionally explored the supermarkets, which fascinated him ("Frankly, I bring back things that Mrs. Eisenhower doesn't know what to do about," he said), sometimes put on an apron to cook for his friends, and often received world leaders who came to seek his advice or simply to pay their respects. Once he sacrificed his treasured privacy to mourn an old friend. On January 30, 1965, Eisenhower led the American delegation at the funeral of Sir Winston Churchill.

In November, 1965, Eisenhower suffered his second and third heart attacks, but the private citizen recovered as the President had done a decade earlier. During the next two years he was hospitalized four times for intestinal ailments. Lumbago and arthritis curtailed his golf game, but in 1968 at Palm Springs he realized the dream of all golfers. He shot a hole in one. It was his last season on the links. On April 29, 1968, he had his fourth heart attack and was flown to the Walter Reed Army Medical Center in Washington for treatment.

Another attack followed on June 15, but by mid-July he was well enough to endorse Richard Nixon for the Presidency. In August he taped an address to the GOP Convention from his hospital bed. That same month he suffered two more heart attacks. Once again he revived, with a resilience that the doctors called little short of remarkable.

On February 23, 1969, Eisenhower underwent surgery to remove scar tissue that was causing an intestinal obstruction. By the middle of March, he had developed congestive heart failure. Finally, at 12:25 P.M. on March 28, Eisenhower's heart failed for the last time. He was seventy-eight years old.

Dwight D. Eisenhower's career, political as well as military, was constantly motivated by a quest for unity. He sat with Presidents Truman and Kennedy at Sam Rayburn's funeral, above, in 1961. In 1968, after a three-hour talk about Vietnam and a round of golf, he relaxed with President Johnson at Palm Springs (far left). Shortly before Eisenhower's death, President Nixon called on him at Walter Reed Army Medical Center.

Eisenhower's coffin lay in state for twenty-eight hours in the Bethlehem Chapel of Washington Cathedral (above) before being taken to the Capitol. It arrived there on an artillery caisson drawn by a team of black horses (left). When the body had been carried into the Rotunda and placed on a bier first used for Lincoln's body in 1865, President Richard Nixon gave the eulogy. Among his listeners were the General's widow and his son, Colonel John Eisenhower (right). During the next twenty-four hours, an estimated 55,000 mourners filed through the Rotunda to pay their respects. Below, General Charles de Gaulle salutes his former comrade-in-arms for the last time.

From the Capitol, Eisenhower's coffin was carried back to Washington Cathedral for a funeral (above) attended by dignitaries from seventy-eight countries. The body was then placed aboard a special train (right) for the forty-hour ride to Abilene, where the General was buried on April 2, 1969.

It was the character of the man—not what he did, but what he was—that so captured the trust and faith and affection of his own people and of the people of the world.

Dwight Eisenhower touched something fundamental in America which only a man of immense force of mind and spirit could have brought so vibrantly alive. He was a product of America's soil, and of its ideals, driven by a compulsion to do right and to do well, a man of deep faith who believed in God and trusted in His will, a man who truly loved his country and for whom words like freedom and democracy were not clichés—but they were living truths.

I know Mrs. Eisenhower would permit me to share with you the last words he spoke to her on the day he died. He said, "I've always loved my wife. I've always loved my children. I've always loved my grandchildren. And I have always loved my country." That was Dwight Eisenhower...

His life reminds us that there is a moral force in this world more powerful than the might of arms, or the wealth of nations. This man who led the most powerful armies that the world has ever seen; this man who led the most powerful nation in the world; this essentially good and gentle and kind man—that moral force was his greatness.

For a quarter of a century to the very end of his life, Dwight Eisenhower exercised a moral authority without parallel in America and in the world. And America and the world is better because of him...

And, so, today we render our final salute. It is a fond salute to a man we loved and cherished. It is a greatful salute to a man whose whole extraordinary life was consecrated to service.

It is a profoundly respectful salute to a man larger than life who by any standard was one of the giants of our time.

—from President Nixon's eulogy for Eisenhower, March 30, 1969

EISENHOWER RECALLED

By MERRIMAN SMITH

Merriman Smith, veteran White House reporter, has been watching Presidents ever since United Press International assigned him to the White House just before Pearl Harbor. He was at Warm Springs when Roosevelt died, he accompanied Truman to Potsdam, and he went on all of Eisenhower's foreign trips. Here, he recalls Eisenhower—the President and the man.

Dwight D. Eisenhower was a complex man who was often underrated by some of his contemporaries. His standing, for example, in the academic and intellectual communities of American political thought was perhaps lower than deserved because liberals regarded him as little more than a smiling figurehead for big business.

He was criticized frequently by liberals for being intellectually lazy and poorly read. This attitude stemmed partly from his well-publicized pastimes—golf and bridge with rich men, watching movies in the White House theatre, and an omnivorous taste for Western novels.

These critics, however, were not familiar with the Eisenhower who could argue fine points of German philosophy learnedly and by the hour. Nor did they realize that behind his generalizations and sometimes hazy and tortured sentences lay a keen knowledge of the world around him.

No President before him or since devoted so much time and effort to personal diplomacy. Eisenhower's extensive foreign tours in the late 1950's proved him to be the most popular man in the world with the possible exception of the late Sir Winston Churchill.

He lived for years in the glory of his World War II command and the Presidency that followed, but for all his popularity and star-spangled record, his White House achievements missed making high marks in history as measured by such recorders as Arthur Schlesinger.

No political leader of recent years left such an imprint on the Republican party. Yet once Eisenhower left office, he was unable to transmit his tremendous popularity to other GOP candidates for the Presidency. Part of this may have been his own fault, for he was not overly energetic on behalf of either Richard M. Nixon in 1960 or Barry Goldwater in 1964.

Republican campaign strategists did not invite Eisenhower into Nixon's 1960 campaign until its closing days. And since the late John F. Kennedy defeated Nixon by such an astonishingly small margin, there is reason to believe that Nixon might have won had Eisenhower campaigned for him earlier that fall.

As for Goldwater, Eisenhower was apprehensive about the Arizona Republican's stand on a number of international matters. In fact, he told this reporter in May of 1964 that he considered Goldwater's foreign policies "dangerous," but,

typically, Eisenhower asked not to be quoted on this matter.

He was about to issue a statement in 1964 supporting Pennsylvania's Governor William Scranton for the Republican nomination, but he changed his mind. He was in Cleveland at the time as the house guest of former Treasury Secretary George M. Humphrey, a Goldwater supporter, and he did not want to embarrass his host. Thus his delay in speaking out for Scranton dealt a serious blow to the Pennsylvanian, who was already bucking almost impossible odds.

The complexity of Eisenhower was no better reflected than in his curious attitude toward politics and politicians. He prided himself, for example, on not being a politician in the conventional sense. He had run for only one office in his life— the Presidency. He either scorned or was bored by some of the wheel horses of his party.

He knew, and this was more factual than arrogant, that a heave of his arms overhead and an ear-to-ear smile could do more for the Republican party than a thousand ward heelers and precinct captains. There were times when he seemed quietly cocky about this. Shortly before leaving the White House he told some dinner guests, "They say I'm not a politician but I will say this—I am a better politician than most of those around me."

During one of our discussions, I told him that a prominent Republican senator had said that given an equal amount of organization, he could take Eisenhower into any major American city and outdraw any figure on the American political scene, including President Lyndon Johnson. We had been talking of the scarcity of Republican presidential timber for 1968. Eisenhower was almost diffident about the generous assessment of his crowd-pulling ability, saying unemotionally, "That may be quite true, but it is unfortunate." His enthusiasm for Nixon, however, soared in 1968. An invalid during that campaign, Ike cheered his former Vice President to victory from a hospital bed.

Looking back on his pre-White House years, it is amazing that he ever entered politics. It was against his thinking and counter to his background. In the late 1940's when he was winding up his tour as Army Chief of Staff, Eisenhower went to the White House to see President Truman. After the conference, reporters gathered around the smiling General in the White House lobby to ask whether he harbored any presidential ambitions. (Some people, including Truman, thought then that Eisenhower was a Democrat.) He took off his cap and plopped down on a leather couch. Speaking almost emotionally, he told his small audience:

"Look, you guys. I don't want to get myself spread all over

the papers with this, but I want you to get something straight. I don't believe a man should ever try to pass his historical peak. I think I pretty well hit my peak in history when I accepted the German surrender in 1945.

"Now, why should I want to get into a completely foreign field and try to top that? Why should I go out and deliberately risk that historical peak by trying to push a bit higher?"

Yet, five years later he decided to do just that after being assured by the politicians of two things: that the country and the party wanted him and that he was a shoo-in for election.

There is some reason to believe that he gave a certain amount of thought to not running for a second term. He had devoted virtually all of his adult life to his country. He and his wife, Mamie, never had a home of their own until they built the Gettysburg house after he became President.

Any serious thoughts he may have had about not running for re-election pretty well vanished after his 1955 heart attack. During his convalescence at Gettysburg, his aides paraded before him frequently the picture of what retirement and vegetation on the farm would be like. He knew the party needed him; that there had been no time to build up a successor, and he also felt that his experience was needed in the increasingly tense cold war. Thus he ran again in 1956 and won another smashing victory over Adlai E. Stevenson.

Eisenhower's cold military logic and his many years of disciplined living helped him survive three major illnesses in the White House. He was an excellent patient in that he followed medical orders precisely and without objection. As far as he was concerned, the doctors were in charge, and it was almost as if it was their heart attack, not his.

When retirement finally came in 1961, Eisenhower went through a period of feeling almost lost in the civilian world. Amazing as it may seem, he did not upon leaving the White House know how to use a dial telephone. He had no driver's license. The world of laundromats, drive-in theatres, bowling alleys, and supermarkets was an utter mystery to him. He began exploring the stores of Gettysburg with avid interest. And it was hard even for those closely associated with him to realize that during his long Army and White House years, most of the everyday chores of living had been done for him, including the placing of telephone calls and driving a car.

When he became accustomed to civilian life, retirement became probably the best years of his life. Until his illness in the fall of 1965, he seemed in many ways to be in better shape than he was in the White House.

I visited with him in Gettysburg on October 11, 1965. Perhaps it may have been somewhat sentimental imagination, but

I thought Eisenhower looked better than he had in years. His acuity and grasp of national and international affairs seemed, if anything, appreciably better than it had been a year or two earlier.

His only physical complaint seemed to be occasional spells of bursitis, which had bothered him for years, and arthritis in his hands, which annoyed him immensely because it interfered at times with his golf grip. He had cut down on golf appreciably and tended to favor the short nine-hole layout at the Augusta National Golf Course over his old favorite, the eighteen-hole Masters Tournament Course.

Highly complicated at times, amazingly simple at others, Eisenhower lived a most satisfying life. Few men of modern times received as many honors. He was an intensely moral person, yet he joined a church for the first time only when he became President. He had an unflagging interest in young people, and he was deeply concerned about the beards, sloppy clothes, and long hairdos of young men as reflective of a lack of self-respect.

A professional soldier, he abhorred fighting. A politician, he scorned connivance for his own part, but he would tolerate a certain amount of it in others. Essentially his world was black and white with very few gray shadings. For example, I once heard him say rather casually that he had never known an entirely honest contractor because men in that business were so subject to the temptations offered by handling large amounts of cash.

Eisenhower was the epitome of personal dignity. Someone once said he was the sort of man who wore a vest to a picnic. Women were delighted by his courtly manners and consideration. Yet he could be strangely barren of consideration or affection for those who worked for him. By and large, they were the troops, and his consideration for them was polite and proper but seldom personal or emotional.

He had a soft streak which he concealed carefully. One of his boyhood friends was ill for several years in a local hospital, and until the man's death, Eisenhower wrote him several letters a week in longhand. Yet he might go months without writing his own brothers.

If ever a man faced death unemotionally and apparently without spoken fear, it was Dwight David Eisenhower. In his orderly way of thinking, he accepted inevitability, and there seemed to be little doubt in his mind that he had devoted an effective lifetime to the service of others.

He was not at all concerned about his critics. He accepted them, too, as part of inevitability. Few men of so many years of leadership could make the same claim to equanimity.

SUPREME HEADQUARTERS
ALLIED EXPEDITIONARY FORCE

Soldiers, Sailors and Airmen of the Allied Expeditionary Force!

You are about to embark upon the Great Crusade, toward which we have striven these many months. The eyes of the world are upon you. The hopes and prayers of liberty-loving people everywhere march with you. In company with our brave Allies and brothers-in-arms on other Fronts, you will bring about the destruction of the German war machine, the elimination of Nazi tyranny over the oppressed peoples of Europe, and security for ourselves in a free world.

Your task will not be an easy one. Your enemy is well trained, well equipped and battle-hardened. He will fight savagely.

But this is the year 1944! Much has happened since the Nazi triumphs of 1940-41. The United Nations have inflicted upon the Germans great defeats, in open battle, man-to-man. Our air offensive has seriously reduced their strength in the air and their capacity to wage war on the ground. Our Home Fronts have given us an overwhelming superiority in weapons and munitions of war, and placed at our disposal great reserves of trained fighting men. The tide has turned! The free men of the world are marching together to Victory!

I have full confidence in your courage, devotion to duty and skill in battle. We will accept nothing less than full Victory!

Good Luck! And let us all beseech the blessing of Almighty God upon this great and noble undertaking.

Dwight Eisenhower

Eisenhower's D-Day message to Allied troops, June 5, 1944

Excerpts from Eisenhower's Speeches and Writings

A CENTURY OF CHALLENGE

The world and we have passed the midway point of a century of continuing challenge. We sense with all our faculties that forces of good and evil are massed and armed and opposed as rarely before in history. This fact defines the meaning of this day. . . .

This trial comes at a moment when man's power to achieve good or to inflict evil surpasses the brightest hopes and the sharpest fears of all ages. We can turn rivers in their courses, level mountains to the plains. Oceans and land and sky are avenues for our colossal commerce. Disease diminishes and life lengthens. Yet the promise of this life is imperiled by the very genius that has made it possible. Nations amass wealth. Labor sweats to create—and turns out devices to level not only mountains but also cities. Science seems ready to confer upon us, as its final gift, the power to erase human life from this planet. At such a time in history, we who are free must proclaim anew our faith. . . .

No person, no home, no community can be beyond the reach of this call. We are summoned to act in wisdom and in conscience, to work with industry, to teach with persuasion, to preach with conviction, to weigh our every deed with care and with compassion. For this truth must be clear before us: whatever America hopes to bring to pass in the world must first come to pass in the heart of America.

—First Inaugural Address,
January 20, 1953

NATIONAL STRENGTH

To be strong nationally is not a sin, it is a necessity! . . . A weakling, particularly a rich and opulent weakling, seeking peaceable solution of a difficulty, is likely to invite contempt; but the same plea from the strong is listened to most respectfully.

—Mandate for Change

POLITICAL LABELS

. . . it would be impossible for me ever to adopt a political philosophy so narrow as to merit the label "liberal," or "conservative," or anything of the sort. I came to believe, as I do to this day, that an individual can only examine and decide for himself each issue . . . in the light of what he believes is good for America as a whole—and let the pundits hang the labels as they may.

—Mandate for Change

ATOMS FOR PEACE

. . . My recital of atomic danger and power is necessarily stated in United States terms, for these are the only incontrovertible facts that I know. I need hardly point out to this assembly, however, that this subject is global, not merely national in character. . . .

If at one time the United States possessed what might have been called a monopoly of atomic power, that monopoly ceased to exist several years ago. Therefore, although our earlier start has permitted us to accumulate what is today a great quantitative advantage, the atomic realities of today comprehend two facts of even greater significance.

First, the knowledge now possessed by several nations will eventually be shared by others, possibly all others.

Second, even a vast superiority in numbers of weapons, and a consequent capability of devastating retaliation, is no preventive, of itself, against the fearful . . . damage and toll of human lives that would be inflicted by surprise aggression. . . .

Should such an atomic attack be launched against the United States, our reaction would be swift and resolute. But for me to say that the defense capabilities of the United States are such that they could inflict terrible losses upon an aggressor—for me to say that the retaliation capabilities of the United States are so great that such an aggressor's land would be laid waste—all this, while fact, is not the true expression of the purpose and the hope of the United States.

To pause there would be to confirm the hopeless finality of a belief that two atomic colossi are doomed malevolently to eye each other indefinitely across a trembling world. To stop there would be to accept helplessly the probability of civilization destroyed—the annihilation of the irreplaceable heritage of mankind handed down to us generation from generation—and the condemnation of mankind to begin all over again the age-old struggle upward from savagery toward decency and right and justice.

Surely no sane member of the human race could discover victory in such desolation. Could anyone wish his name to be coupled by history with such human degradation? . . .

In this quest, I know that we must not lack patience.

I know that in a world divided, such as ours today, salvation cannot be attained by one dramatic act.

I know that many steps will have to be taken over many months before the world can look at itself one day and truly realize that a new climate of mutually peaceful confidence is abroad in the world. . . . But . . . the gravity of the time is such that every new avenue of peace, no matter how dimly discernible, should be explored.

There is at least one new avenue of peace which has not yet

been well explored—an avenue now laid out by the General Assembly of the United Nations.

In its resolution of Nov. 18, 1953, this General Assembly suggested—and I quote—"that the Disarmament Commission study the desirability of establishing a subcommittee consisting of representatives of the powers principally involved, which should seek, in private, an acceptable solution—and report such a solution to the General Assembly and to the Security Council not later than 1 September, 1954."

The United States, heeding the suggestion of the General Assembly of the United Nations, is instantly prepared to meet privately with such other countries as may be "principally involved," to seek "an acceptable solution" to the atomic armaments race which overshadows not only the peace but the very life of the world.

We shall carry into these private or diplomatic talks a new conception. The United States would seek more than the mere reduction or elimination of atomic materials for military purposes.

It is not enough to take this weapon out of the hands of the soldiers. It must be put into the hands of those who will know how to strip its military casing and adapt it to the arts of peace. . . .

I would be prepared to submit to the Congress of the United States, and with every expectation of approval, any such plan that would:

First, encourage world-wide investigation into the most effective peacetime uses of fissionable material;

Second, begin to diminish the potential destructive power of the world's atomic stockpiles;

Third, allow all peoples of all nations to see that, in this enlightened age, the great powers of the earth, both of the East and of the West, are interested in human aspirations first rather than in building up the armaments of war.

Fourth, open up a new channel for peaceful discussion and initiate at least a new approach to the many difficult problems that must be solved in both private and public conversations if the world is to shake off the inertia imposed by fear and is to make positive progress toward peace.

Against the dark background of the atomic bomb, the United States does not wish merely to present strength, but also the desire and the hope for peace.

The coming months will be fraught with fateful decisions. In this Assembly, in the capitals and military headquarters of the world; in the hearts of men everywhere, be they governed or governors, may they be the decisions which will lead this world out of fear and into peace. . . .

—Address at the United Nations,
December 8, 1953

SPIRIT OF GENEVA

We cannot expect here, in the few hours of a few days, to solve all the problems of all the world that need to be solved. Indeed, the four of us meeting here have no authority from others that could justify us even in attempting that. The roots of many of these problems are buried deep in wars, conflicts, and history. They are made even more difficult by the differences in governmental ideologies and ambitions. Manifestly it is out of the question in the short time available to the heads of government meeting here to trace out the causes and origins of these problems and to devise agreements that could, with complete fairness to all, eliminate them.

Nevertheless, we can, perhaps, create a new spirit that will make possible future solutions of problems which are within our responsibilities. And equally important we can try to take here and now at Geneva the first steps on a new road to a just and durable peace. . . .

—Address at the opening of the Geneva Conference,
July 18, 1955

MAN IN THE WHITE HOUSE

The man in the White House, I believe, should think of himself as President of all the people. Even though a party's nominee in a national election might lose every state in a major geographical region, he should not neglect the opportunity during the campaign to learn more about the problems and attitudes of that region to make his own ideas and proposals affecting the nation known there.

—Mandate for Change

THE CROSS OF IRON

Today the hope of free men remains stubborn and brave, but it is sternly disciplined by experience. It shuns not only all crude counsel of despair but also the self-deceit of easy illusion. It weighs the chance for peace with sure, clear knowledge of what happened to the vain hope of 1945.

In that spring of victory the soldiers of the Western Allies met the soldiers of Russia in the center of Europe. They were triumphant comrades in arms. Their people shared the joyous prospect of building, in honor of their dead, the only fitting monument—an age of just peace. . . .

This comman purpose lasted an instant and perished. The nations of the world divided to follow two distinct roads.

The United States and our valued friends, the other free nations, chose one road.

The leaders of the Soviet Union chose another. . . . The amassing of Soviet power alerted free nations to a new danger of aggression. It compelled them in self-defense to spend unprecedented money and energy for armaments. It forced them to develop weapons of war now capable of inflicting instant and terrible punishment upon any aggressor.

It instilled in the free nations—and let none doubt this—the unshakable conviction that, as long as there persists a threat to freedom, they must, at any cost, remain armed, strong, and ready for the risk of war. . . . The free nations, most solemnly and repeatedly, have assured the Soviet Union that their firm association has never had any aggressive purpose whatsoever. Soviet leaders, however, have seemed to persuade themselves, or tried to persuade their people, otherwise.

And so it has come to pass that the Soviet Union itself has shared and suffered the very fears it had fostered in the rest of the world. This has been the way of life forged by eight years of fear and force. What can the world, or any nation in it, hope for if no turning is found on this dread road?

The worst to be feared and the best to be expected can be simply stated. The *worst* is atomic war.

The *best* would be this: a life of perpetual fear and tension; a burden of arms draining the wealth and the labor of all peoples; a wasting of strength that defies the American system or the Soviet system or any system to achieve true abundance and happiness for the peoples of this earth.

Every gun that is made, every warship launched, every rocket fired signifies, in the final sense, a theft from those who hunger and are not fed, those who are cold and are not clothed.

This world in arms is not spending money alone.

It is spending the sweat of its laborers, the genius of its scientists, the hopes of its children.

The cost of one modern heavy bomber is this: a modern brick school in more than thirty cities. . . .

We pay for a single fighter plane with a half million bushels of wheat.

We pay for a single destroyer with new homes that could have housed more than eight thousand people.

This, I repeat, is the best way of life to be found on the road the world has been taking.

This is not a way of life at all, in any true sense. Under the cloud of threatening war, it is humanity hanging from a cross of iron. . . .

This Government is ready to ask its people to join with all nations in devoting a substantial percentage of the savings achieved by disarmament to a fund for world aid and reconstruction. The purposes of this great work would be to help other peoples to develop the underdeveloped areas of the world, to stimulate profitable and fair world trade, to assist all peoples to know the blessings of production freedom. . . .

If we strive but fail and the world remains armed against itself, it at least need be divided no longer in its clear knowledge of who has condemned humankind to this fate. . . . These proposals spring, without ulterior purpose or political passion, from our calm conviction that the hunger for peace is in the hearts of all peoples—those of Russia and of China no less than of our own country. . . . They aspire to this: the lifting, from the backs and from the hearts of men, of their burden of arms and of fears, so that they may find before them a golden age of freedom and of peace. . . .

—*Address to the American Society of Newspaper Editors,
April 16, 1953*

THE SYMBOL OF HUMAN FORCES

Humility must always be the portion of any man who receives acclaim earned in the blood of his followers and the sacrifices of his friends. . . . The only attitude in which a commander may with satisfaction receive the tributes of his friends is in humble acknowledgment that, no matter how unworthy he may be, his position is a symbol of great human forces that have labored arduously and successfully for a righteous cause. Unless he feels this symbolism and this rightness in what he has tried to do, then he is disregardful of the courage, the fortitude and devotion of the vast multitudes he has been honored to command. If all the Allied men and women that have served with me in this war can only know that it is they this august body is really honoring today, then, indeed, will I be content.

—*Address at Guildhall, London,
June 12, 1945*

THE MILITARY-INDUSTRIAL COMPLEX

Until the latest of our world conflicts, the United States had no armaments industry. American makers of plowshares could, with time and as required, make swords as well. But now we can no longer risk emergency improvisation of national defense; we have been compelled to create a permanent armaments industry of vast proportions. . . . This conjunction of an immense military establishment and a large arms industry is new in the American experience. . . . We recognize the imperative need for this development. Yet we must not fail to comprehend its grave implications. . . .

In the councils of government we must guard against the acquisition of unwarranted influence, whether sought or unsought, by the military-industrial complex. The potential for the disastrous rise of misplaced power exists and will persist. We must never let the weight of this combination endanger our liberties or democratic processes. . . .

—*Farewell Address,
January 17, 1961*

Chronological Summary of the Life of Dwight David Eisenhower

1890

Born David Dwight Eisenhower (known as Dwight David from early childhood), Denison, Texas, October 14, to Ida and David Eisenhower

1891

Moves with family to Abilene, Kansas

1909

Graduates from high school

1911

Enters United States Military Academy at West Point

1915

Graduates from West Point, 61st in a class of 164; commissioned as second lieutenant; assigned to 19th Infantry Regiment, Fort Sam Houston, Texas

1916

Promoted to first lieutenant; marries Mamie Geneva Doud in Denver, Colorado, July 1

1917

Assigned as regimental supply officer of the 57th Infantry, Leon Springs, Texas, promoted to captain (permanent) in May; then transferred to Fort Oglethorpe, Georgia, as instructor in Officers Training Camp, and later to Fort Leavenworth as instructor at Army Service Schools. First son, Doud Dwight, born September 24 (died January 2, 1921)

1918

Ordered to Camp Meade, Maryland, to organize the 65th Battalion Engineers; then to Tank Training Center at Camp Colt, Gettysburg, as commanding officer; promoted to major (temporary) in June; promoted to lieutenant colonel (temporary) in October

1919

Ordered to Camp Meade to command a succession of heavy tank battalions

1920

Reverts to captain (permanent) in June and promoted to major (permanent) in July

1921

Graduates from Tank School at Camp Meade, in command of the 301st Tank Battalion

1922

Becomes executive officer for the 20th Infantry Brigade in Panama Canal Zone. Second son, John Sheldon Doud, born August 3

1924

Returns to United States and becomes recreation officer for Third Corps Area in Baltimore, Maryland; then recruiting officer at Fort Logan, Colorado, in December

1925

Attends Command and General Staff School at Fort Leavenworth in Kansas

1926

Graduates from Command and General Staff School, first in his class; becomes executive officer for 24th Infantry at Fort Benning, Georgia

1927

Assigned to the American Battle Monuments Commission in Washington, D.C., to prepare guidebook on European battlefields of World War I

1928

Graduates from Army War College in Washington, D.C.; is sent to France by Battle Monuments Commission; receives Distinguished Service Medal for work at Camp Colt

1929

Returns to Washington, D.C., becomes assistant executive in the office of Assistant Secretary of War, attends Army Industrial College

1933

Assigned to be assistant to General Douglas MacArthur, Chief of Staff, United States Army

1935

Named senior assistant to General MacArthur, Military Adviser of the Commonwealth of the Philippines; receives pilot's license

1936

Promoted to lieutenant colonel (permanent)

1939

Leaves Philippines for San Francisco in December

1940

Joins 15th Infantry Regiment in February as executive officer, located first at Fort Ord, California, and then in March at Fort Lewis in Washington; becomes Chief of Staff of Third Division at Fort Lewis

1941

Made Chief of Staff for Ninth Army Corps at Fort Lewis; promoted to colonel (temporary); made Chief of Staff for Lieutenant General Walter Krueger, Commander of the Third

Army at Fort Sam Houston, Texas; promoted to brigadier general (temporary); assigned to Washington, D.C., Assistant Chief of Staff, War Plans Division

1942

Named Assistant Chief of Staff, in charge of War Plans; father dies in March; promoted to major general (temporary); named Assistant Chief of Staff, in charge of New Operations Division; arrives in London in May to study joint defense; appointed Commander of the European Theater of Operations on June 15; promoted to lieutenant general (temporary) in July; commands the Allied invasion of North Africa on November 8

1943

Promoted to temporary rank of full general; completes invasion of North Africa in May; directs invasion of Sicily in July and August; promoted to brigadier general (permanent) and major general (permanent) on August 30; launches Italian campaign in September; confers with Roosevelt at Oran on November 19; attends Cairo Conference on November 22; appointed Supreme Commander of Allied Expeditionary Forces on December 24

1944

Arrives in London in January to establish Supreme Headquarters; directs Normandy invasion on June 6; appointed General of the Army (temporary)

1945

Accepts unconditional surrender of Germany at Rheims on May 7; makes speech at Guildhall in London on June 12; appears before joint session of Congress on June 18; dissolves Supreme Headquarters of the Allied Expeditionary Forces in July; becomes commander of United States occupation zone of Germany and U.S. representative on the Allied Control Council; returns to Washington, D.C., as Chief of Staff of the U.S. Army, November 19

1946

Promoted to General of the Army, Regular Army (date of rank—December 20, 1944) on April 11

1948

Resigns as Chief of Staff on May 2; installed as President of Columbia University on October 12 and is engaged as senior military adviser to Secretary of Defense James Forrestal; publishes *Crusade In Europe*

1950

Appointed Supreme Commander of North Atlantic Treaty Organization, December 18

1952

Announces availability as Republican candidate for President in January; relieved as commander of North Atlantic Treaty Organization in June; nominated for President by Republicans, July 11; defeats Adlai E. Stevenson on November 4; visits Korea in December

1953

Inaugurated 34th President of the United States, January 20; attends Bermuda Conference in December with Churchill and French Premier Laniel; delivers "Atoms for Peace" speech at the United Nations, December 8

1955

Attends Geneva Summit Conference in July with Eden, Bulganin, and French Premier Faure; suffers heart attack on September 24

1956

Announces in February he will run for second term; attends meeting of Presidents of the Americas in Panama, July 21; wins presidential election in November

1957

Seeks acceptance of Eisenhower Doctrine (economic and military aid to Middle East) before Congress, January 5; orders United States troops to Little Rock to uphold Federal court order on school desegregation; meets with North Atlantic Treaty Organization leaders in Paris in December

1959

Visits West Germany, France, and England in support of Atlantic Alliance in July; in December visits eleven Asian, European, and African countries

1960

Visits Alaska, Philippines, Taiwan, Okinawa, and Hawaii

1961

Retires to Gettysburg farm; publishes *Peace with Justice*

1963

Publishes *Mandate for Change*

1965

Heads American delegation at Churchill's funeral, January 30; suffers two heart attacks; publishes *Waging Peace*

1968

Suffers four heart attacks; strongly endorses Richard M. Nixon for the Presidency

1969

Dies on March 28 in Walter Reed Army Medical Center in Washington, D.C., at the age of seventy-eight

A NOTE ON THIS BOOK

This book was produced jointly by United Press International and American Heritage Publishing Co., Inc., under the following editorial direction: for United Press International, Roger Tatarian, Vice President and Editor, and Harold Blumenfeld, Executive Newspictures Editor; for American Heritage Publishing Co., Inc., Richard M. Ketchum, Managing Director of the Book Division, and Irwin Glusker, Senior Art Director.

The staff for this book was as follows: Editor, Charles L. Mee, Jr.; Designers, Ken Munowitz, Jack Newman, and Peter Saladino; Assistant Editors, Deborah Aronsohn, Patricia Frome, and Nancy Simon; Copy Editor, Elaine Andrews; Editorial Assistants, George Horwitz, Sara Hunter, and Muriel Vrotsos.

All pictures, except as otherwise credited, come from the files of UPI.

The cover picture is a formal portrait of General Eisenhower, taken in 1951 while he served as Supreme Allied Commander in Europe.

Picture credits: Birnback Publishing Service (Ullstein), 38–39. Culver Pictures, Inc., 8 top left. Cushing Agency, Charles Phelps, 6–7. Dickinson County Historical Society, 13 top. Eisenhower Museum, 8 bottom, 12–13, 13 bottom, 15, 24 top and bottom, 28–29 left top and bottom. European Picture Service, 41. Fox Photos, Ltd., 40. Free Lance Photographers Guild, 97. The Grange Collection, 8 top right. Harris & Ewing, 101 top. Imperial War Museum, London, 44, 66–67 middle left. Warren Josephy Collection, 140. Library of Congress, 42. Magnum, Robert Capa, 64–65, 66–67 top, 66–67 bottom right (*Images of War*, © 1964), 68 bottom. Magnum, Burt Glinn, 129. Magnum, Sergio Larrain, 118 middle left, 118 bottom left, 118 bottom right. Magnum, Wayne Miller, 119. National Maritime Museum, Greenwich, England, 30–31. New York Public Library, 16. Robert Phillips, 120 top. Winter Prather, 17 both, 18 both, 19 all, 20 both, 21 both, 72. Franklin D. Roosevelt Library, Hyde Park, N.Y., 52. Frank Scherschel, *Life* Magazine © Time, Inc., 62–63. Brian Seed, 58–59. Shostal, Harvey Hament, 112. George Tames, New York *Times*, 105, 128, 136–37. U.S. Army Photographs, 29 top right, 45, 46–47, 48–49, 50–51 both, 60–61, 66–67 bottom left, 67 middle right, 68 middle, 70–71, 78–79, 82–83. United States Military Academy, West Point, 22–23. Map 106 top, Argenziano Associates. Drawings by Burt Silverman.